Johnsons

Your baby's
FIRST YEAR

LONDON, NEW YORK, MUNICH, MELBOURNE, DELHI

First published in Great Britain in 2005 by
Dorling Kindersley, A Penguin Company
80 Strand, London WC2R 0RL

The information in this book was previously published in 2004 within the
following titles in the JOHNSON'S® Everyday Babycare series:
JOHNSON'S® *Breastfeeding*
JOHNSON'S® *Sleep*
JOHNSON'S® *Crying & Comforting*
JOHNSON'S® *Feeding Your Baby*
JOHNSON'S® *Baby & Child Safety*
JOHNSON'S® *Learning to Talk*

2 4 6 8 10 9 7 5 3 1

Every effort has been made to ensure that the information contained in this book is complete and
accurate. However, neither the publisher nor the author are engaged in rendering professional
advice or services to the individual reader. The ideas, procedures and suggestions contained in this
book are not intended as a substitute for consulting with your healthcare provider. All matters
regarding the health of you and your baby require medical supervision. Neither the author nor the
publisher shall be liable or responsible for any loss or damage allegedly arising from any
information or suggestion in this book.

A CIP catalogue record for this book is available from the British Library

ISBN 1 4053 0749 8

Reproduced by Colourscan, Singapore
Printed by Star Standard, Singapore

See our complete catalogue at
www.dk.com

A message to parents from

Johnson's®

The most precious gift in the world is a new baby. To your little one, you are the centre of the universe. And by following your most basic instincts to touch, hold and talk to your baby, you provide the best start to a happy, healthy life.

Our baby products encourage parents to care for and nurture their children through the importance of touch, developing a deep, loving bond that transcends all others.

Parenting is not an exact science, nor is it a one-size-fits-all formula. For more than a hundred years, Johnson & Johnson has supported the healthcare needs of parents and healthcare professionals, and we understand that all parents feel more confident in their role when they have information they can trust.

That is why we offer this book as our commitment to you to provide scientifically sound, professionally reviewed guidance on the important topics of pregnancy, babycare and child development.

As you read through this book, the most important thing to remember is this: you know your baby better than anyone else. By watching, listening and having confidence in your natural ability, you will know how to use the information you have in your hands, for the benefit of the baby in your arms.

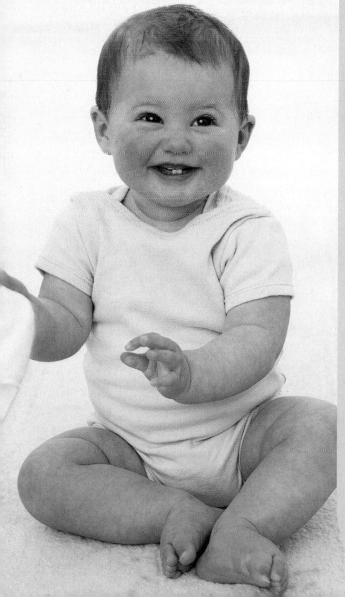

contents

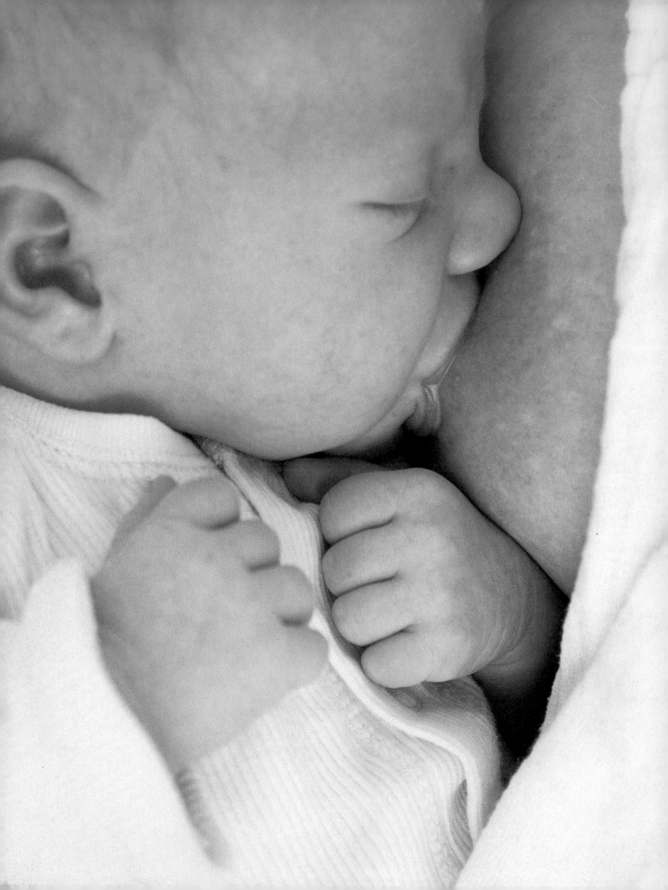

0-3
months

" I didn't realize I'd enjoy caring for Sam so much. We have our **bonding time** together every day. **"**

SARAH, mother of six-week-old Sam

" Ben is a gorgeous, healthy baby – he **positively glows** with health. I love watching him at the breast and thinking to myself, that's **pure goodness.** "

ELLEN, mother of six-week-old Ben

The benefits of breastfeeding

Breastfeeding will give your baby the best possible start in life. Wherever you are, whatever your circumstances, whether you've given birth to a full-term baby or one who is premature – breastfeeding is a gift that's yours, and yours alone, to give to your child.

Benefits for your baby

Breast milk is the perfect food for your baby because it has been developed and designed with him in mind, over thousands of years. However good formula milk is – and it's true to say that it is better now than it's ever been – it can at best only mimic breast milk, and will never be as good as the real thing. Why? Because breast milk is packed with the exact nutrients a human baby needs. It also contains living antibodies from your body that help protect your baby from disease.

For hundreds of years, all over the world, people have understood that breast milk protects babies as well as helping them to grow. Over recent years, doctors and scientists have carried out studies to show exactly how strong the protection offered by breast milk is, and more studies are being carried out all the time. These studies have all reached the same conclusion: breastfeeding protects your child against illness, both in the first few months of life and during the childhood years beyond.

- Breastfed babies are at far lower risk of gastrointestinal illnesses, which are responsible for the hospitalization of a sizeable number of babies every year.
- Exclusive breastfeeding protects against respiratory illness: a study into this found babies who were bottle-fed, or combined breast and bottle, ran twice the risk of getting a lung or respiratory tract infection of some kind.
- Urinary tract infections are less common among breastfed babies;

bottle-fed babies were found to be at five times higher risk of these.
- Ear infections are less common among breastfed babies.
- A Scandinavian study suggests breastfeeding offers some protection against Sudden Infant Death Syndrome (SIDS).

Research results

Studies show that breastfed babies reach their milestones quicker than other babies.

In particular they seem to:

- learn to crawl earlier
- learn to speak sooner
- have a higher IQ – babies breastfed for between seven and nine months have higher intelligence on average than those breastfed for less than seven months.

Research has also shown that breastfeeding boosts your baby's immune system in ways that give him long-term protection as he's growing up.

• A child who was breastfed is less likely than one who was bottle-fed to get respiratory illness up to the age of seven.

• There's some long-term protection against gastrointestinal illnesses.

• Breastfeeding reduces the risk of developing either asthma and eczema.

• There's a lower risk of childhood diabetes and leukaemia if a baby has been breastfed.

• A child who was breastfed is less likely to be obese than one who was bottle-fed.

One study found that children born prematurely seem to benefit from being fed breast milk in the early weeks of life (see pages 65–67): they had an 8.3 point IQ advantage over premature babies who hadn't been fed breast milk. Full-term babies who'd been breastfed for four months or less had

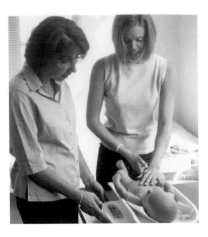

ON THE SCALES
Most healthy full-term babies don't need weighing too often: you'll know your baby is feeding well and growing if he is perky and produces plenty of wet nappies.

a 3.7 point IQ lead on those who'd been bottle-fed. It's thought these IQ advantages are due to the long-chain polyunsaturated fatty acids in breast milk that encourage brain development. Other studies have found that breastfed babies tend to crawl and improve their fine motor skills earlier than bottle-fed babies.

Expert tip

Breastfeeding prepares a baby's jaw and mouth muscles for speech. Anecdotally, many health visitors report that breastfed babies speak earlier than bottle-fed infants – it is thought that feeding from a nipple strengthens more muscles in the face and jaw than feeding from a teat.

Will breastfeeding help me bond with my baby?

Breastfeeding a baby is one of the most intimate human experiences: you and your baby are wrapped, tummy to tummy, in a warm and lengthy embrace. It's a wonderful, nature-given opportunity to enjoy being at one with this remarkable little person who's spent so long inside your body. Breastfeeding is the perfect way to bond with your baby.

The love hormone

That isn't to say that women who don't choose to breastfeed don't bond with their babies, or that every breastfeed will be an idyllic experience. But when breastfeeding is going well it is undoubtedly a special bonding time with your baby.

Oxytocin, one of the hormones released in the mother during breastfeeding, is known as the "love hormone". Scientists believe that oxytocin primes a new mother to love her baby and to bond with him. It is nature's way of ensuring that new babies are loved and cared for, right from the start.

Make time to bond

Whether you are breast- or bottle-feeding, bonding doesn't necessarily happen immediately after the birth. Learning to love your baby may take a few hours or days or even weeks. The secret is to learn to relax. Make time to bond. If you're back at home, go to bed with your baby for a day or two and spend some uninterrupted time together, if you can. Remember that breastfeeding isn't just about

getting enough milk in: it's about pouring love into your baby, too. While you're feeding him, think about how the world looks from his point of view. You are everything to him.

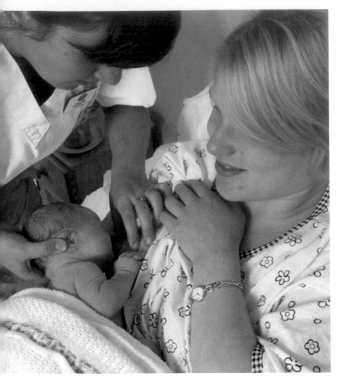

LEARNING HOW TO LATCH ON *Make sure you learn early on how to position your baby correctly and ensure a good latch – this will pay dividends later.*

suggest that if you don't have a "successful" breastfeed within a certain time of the birth breastfeeding will suffer. The best advice is to take things easy, relax, and believe that both you and your baby will get the hang of it in time. And you will.

Your hospital stay

There are pros and cons to your hospital stay. On the up side, if you do need any help to breastfeed there are trained health workers all around who will support and advise you. However, if you're on a postnatal ward you may be surrounded by other new mothers and their babies. This can mean like-minded people to talk to, but it can also mean having to put up with other babies' crying, and lots of people coming and going.

Getting expert advice

It's a good idea to use the time of your hospital stay to get some expert input on your breastfeeding technique. Often you'll be visited by a lactation specialist as a matter of routine, but, if not, ask to see her. And if you've got any questions on your baby's feeding and growth that a doctor could help with, make a point of talking to the paediatrician before you're discharged.

Many new mothers worry about the amount of milk, or colostrum,

What is colostrum?

Colostrum is the milk your breasts produce during the first few days after the birth – unlike mature milk, which is thinner-looking, colostrum is creamy and thick. It's loaded with protein, a small amount of fat and carbohydrates, and best of all it's incredibly easy for a baby to digest. So, although you may feel you aren't making a huge volume of milk, remember that what you are making is full of goodness. Colostrum is also full of antibodies, including some new ones that the baby hasn't had in the womb.

The first feed

Studies show that the earlier breastfeeding starts, the easier it's likely to be. If possible, make sure the health professionals who are with you for the birth know you want to be able to put your baby to the breast as soon as possible after she's born. Don't worry if your baby doesn't immediately latch on. It's great if this does happen, but it really doesn't mean you're doomed to failure if she doesn't – far from it. Many babies are simply too interested in the big new world around them to start breastfeeding straight away. There's no research to

they seem to be producing in the early days. It's true that for the first two or three days after the birth your milk, or colostrum, won't be great in volume, but this is because newborn babies don't need a lot of liquid. They're born with reserves of water – the loss of this is what causes the traditional dip in their weight in the days after birth – but what they really do need is the antibody protection of breast milk.

Leaving hospital

In hospital you'll have had 24-hour help with breastfeeding from medical staff. If you've called on them for a lot of support, you may find the idea of leaving to go home daunting. Many women, though, find breastfeeding gets easier when they're back in their own surroundings – it's easier to relax and be comfortable in your own home.

It's important once you leave hospital to know where you could go to for help and support if you do need it. Call an advisor at the first hint of a problem.

Get help if you have a tender lump in your breast, are feeling feverish, or there is a red patch on your breast. These are all signs of a possible blocked milk duct, which could lead to mastitis (see page 21), but with help right away it should be prevented.

Your emotions

In the days after the birth you may feel tired and emotional a lot of the time - common problems can seem overwhelming. This is normal and almost all mothers remember going through something similar.

Persevere and try to believe things will improve – it might help to talk to another woman who remembers what everything felt like in the early days. It's important, too, to have the support of someone you trust – perhaps your midwife, or a health visitor, or a breastfeeding advisor. Decide whose support you most value and listen to that one person.

Breastfeeding twins

- Beware visitors who might be negative about your ability to breastfeed two babies. You're perfectly capable of feeding your twins: breastfeeding works on the supply and demand principle, so two babies sucking produces enough milk for both!

- Breastfeeding both the babies together will save you a lot of time. But you'll probably sometimes want to feed them one by one, to help you bond with them individually.

- A good way to feed both is to use the football hold (see right and page 15). Or lie them in front of you with their legs overlapping, making an X shape in your lap.

- Use lots of pillows so you're comfortable - you may find it worthwhile investing in a V-shaped cushion.

- Alternate feeding each baby from both breasts - this evens out their needs and prevents you getting lopsided if one baby feeds more than the other.

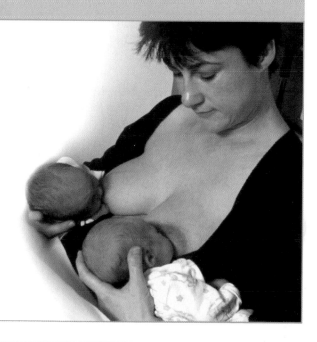

How do I position my baby?

Good positioning is crucial to happy and contented breastfeeding. Not only does it ensure that you and your baby are comfortable, and help you avoid sore nipples, it also helps the milk to flow properly and your baby to suck more efficiently. Take as much time as you need to make sure your baby is positioned correctly.

CRADLE HOLD
This is the classic breastfeeding position. Make sure your baby's face and entire body are turned towards your breast – her head should be lying on the fleshy part of your arm. Alternatively, you can support her head with your opposite arm.

Latching on

Wait until your baby's mouth is open really wide before you move her close to the nipple, and always bring your baby to your breast, never your breast to your baby. Signs that you've got a good latch include:

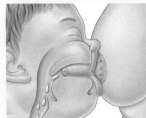

★ your baby's lower lip is curled back underneath your nipple

★ your baby's ears move as she sucks

★ you feel no pain at all or only a slight pain as she starts to suck (if it's very painful, take her off the breast and reposition her, as a bad latch will cause sore nipples).

Make yourself comfortable

Always make sure you're feeling comfortable before you start a feed. If possible, in the early days, get someone else to hold the baby while you sit down and sort yourself out. Have plenty of cushions or pillows handy – you might like to use them to lie the baby on.

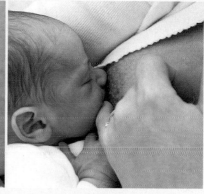

ROOTING
Brush your newborn's upper lip with your nipple to coax her to open her mouth wide enough to get a good latch.

ENSURING A GOOD LATCH
If you are at all unsure about your baby's position or latch, ease her off the breast and start again.

COMING OFF THE BREAST
Slide your little finger into the corner of your baby's mouth to break the seal it forms around your breast.

Once your baby is in a feeding position, use your free hand to support your breast to offer it to her. This is especially important in the early days, since your breasts will be full and heavy – latching on will soon become easier and you won't think twice about it, but right now you need to give it your full attention.

Cup your free hand around your nipple in what's called the C hold – this means you'll have your four fingers underneath your nipple and your thumb on top, making the shape of a letter C. Keep your fingers well back from the areola, and don't squeeze it too tightly or you may constrict the milk ducts – you're guiding the nipple to your baby's mouth, not squeezing the milk into her.

Different positions

Alternatives to the traditional cradle hold (opposite) include lying down to feed (right) and the football hold (a good position to try in the early days as it gives you more control over the baby's head).

Women who have had a Caesarean section may also find it particularly comfortable as it keeps the baby's weight off the scar. Use a pillow or cushion to support your baby's body, and tuck her trunk and legs in under your arm, with her head in your hand.

LYING DOWN TO FEED
This is a great way to feed, especially after a Caesarean. Lie on your side with your baby facing your breast. Keep her head level with your breast so she doesn't have to pull or reach for your nipple. Her body should be tucked well in against your side.

Questions & Answers

My baby is two days old, and my nipples are really sore. What should I do?

You need help with getting the positioning right (see pages 14–15). Ask a midwife or breastfeeding counsellor to come along and give you some advice. If one side is less sore than the other, feed from that side first – once the milk is flowing the pain will lessen. Expressing a little milk from the sore breast will also help ease the pain.

My breasts are rock-solid and uncomfortable. Why is this?

This is common in the days after the birth – your breasts are over-producing because they don't know how much milk your baby needs. Things will settle down in time. Until then, use a warm compress on your breast before feeding – this will help the let-down reflex. Between feeds use a cold compress or ice pack to help relieve swelling and pain. Some women find that putting a cold cabbage leaf inside their bra helps relieve discomfort.

My milk spurts out so fast the baby seems almost choked by it! Should I be worried by this?

It's quite common to have a lot of milk in the early days after giving birth because your body hasn't yet "learned" how much it needs to make, so to compensate it's over-producing. Things will soon start to settle down over the next few days and weeks.

Back at home

The big plus to stepping over your own threshold with your baby in your arms is that, finally, you can properly relax in your own bed with your familiar things all around you. Make the most of it: pamper yourself, and lap up every bit of pampering offered by your partner.

Breastfeeding works best when you can focus on your baby as much as possible. Obviously you'll want your partner to be fully involved in the early hours and days with her, but also find quiet times when you can concentrate on your baby to feed.

Later on you'll be able to breastfeed amid almost any hurly-burly, but the process of getting breastfeeding going will be smoother if you're able to devote your attention fully to your baby as you're feeding.

These early days once you're back home are sometimes called your babymoon period: it's the time when you can nestle down and simply enjoy being together – you, your baby and your partner. Friends and family will phone and want to rush around to see the baby – but, despite part of you being keen to show her off, try to hold back from too many

WINDING
Winding helps your baby get rid of any air she has taken in while feeding: a rub on the back or a gentle pat is usually all that's needed.

After a Caesarean section

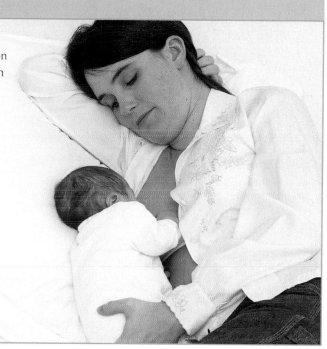

If you've had a Caesarean section you may face extra challenges in starting to breastfeed, but there's no reason to think you won't be able to do it. To begin with, both you and your baby may still feel a little woozy from the effects of the drugs you had, but try to be patient because these will wear off. Your milk will come in as normal and you will soon become as expert at breastfeeding as any other mother.

If over the first few days your scar is painful, try using the relaxation techniques you learned during your antenatal classes to help you relax.

These positions may also help:

- lying down (see page 15)

- lying your baby on a V-shaped cushion which protects your scar while she feeds

- sitting up in bed – if this isn't too painful – with lots of pillows across your knees to support the baby.

visitors all at once. Remember that you'll have plenty of time, in the weeks and months ahead, to share this new little person with her wider circle. For the moment, what's crucial for you both – and for your future breastfeeding – is that you take time to focus on one another, and on getting breastfeeding right.

Remember to talk to your baby while you're feeding her. Tell her how well she's doing – whisper to her how much you love her. It isn't just milk you are pouring into her little body – it's love as well. And that's every bit as important in helping her grow big and strong.

How often should I feed?

It's common to worry about how often and for how long your baby feeds. However, it's best to resist trying to gauge how much milk your baby takes from you.

- Most babies will stop suckling, fall asleep or just release the breast when they have had enough. Experts do not recommend timing your baby's feeds, but allow her to regulate her own feed by coming off the first breast on her own. Then you can burp her and offer the second side. Some babies will nurse 10 minutes a side, others 30. As she nurses longer she will get more of the hindmilk,

which is higher in fat, giving her a feeling of fullness, and she will release the breast or fall asleep.

- Alternate which breast your baby starts on to keep up your milk supply.

Expert tip

It's very important that your baby keeps up her intake of fluids – dehydration is a serious condition in a small baby, and it can take hold very quickly. If your baby stops being interested in feeding, seems floppy, has a dry mouth or eyes, is producing few wet nappies or has diarrhoea or frequent vomiting, get medical help straight away.

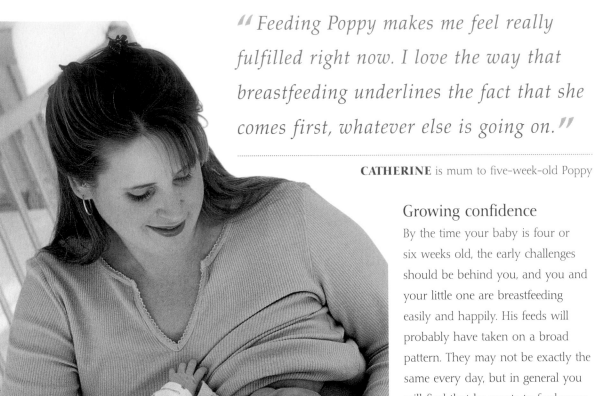

"Feeding Poppy makes me feel really fulfilled right now. I love the way that breastfeeding underlines the fact that she comes first, whatever else is going on."

CATHERINE is mum to five-week-old Poppy

Growing confidence

By the time your baby is four or six weeks old, the early challenges should be behind you, and you and your little one are breastfeeding easily and happily. His feeds will probably have taken on a broad pattern. They may not be exactly the same every day, but in general you will find that he wants to feed more and to sleep more, usually in the morning. He gradually has smaller feeds, and longer wakeful periods, as the day wears on.

As time goes by this pattern will probably evolve further, until his

Is my baby getting enough milk?

This is a common question and there are plenty of clues as to whether your baby is getting enough milk. Look out for:

● six to eight wet nappies over a 24-hour period

● yellow stools – it doesn't matter if you get several dirty nappies a day or one every few days; in general babies older than a month will start to go for longer periods without passing a stool

● gradual weight gain, although this is not necessarily even, and a dropping-off of weight gain should not be taken in isolation to suggest that feeding isn't going well

● your baby being generally alert, bright-eyed, interested in what's going on around him

● a feeling of softer, less heavy breasts after your baby has fed.

If these indicators seem to fit you and your baby, you can relax because breastfeeding is going just fine!

naps consolidate by around the age of seven months into a morning nap and an afternoon nap – one of these, often the morning one, will be longer. You'll find your baby will want to feed before and often after a nap, although the post-nap feed may be little more than a quick pick-me-up and he'll soon neglect that as he grows older.

How many feeds should my baby have a day?

It's sometimes said that the best approach to breastfeeding is not to count your baby's breastfeeds at all: breastfeeding is difficult to quantify, and it's almost impossible to estimate how much milk your baby is taking in. Having said that, research shows that babies tend to have between eight and 12 feeds a day, and paediatricians do sometimes suggest a mother counts her baby's feeds over a 24-hour period to check the feeds are in this sort of region. Too many feeds, over a consistent period, may suggest the baby isn't feeding as efficiently as he could; too few feeds could mean he needs to spend more time at the breast to up his intake.

Growth spurts

Yesterday your baby was blissfully happy – today he wants to feed all day! He may be having a growth or appetite spurt, so his body needs more milk and he needs to communicate the fact to your breasts. He does so by sucking more than usual, which tells your body to produce more milk, and it will do in the coming days.

Your body almost certainly can provide enough milk for your baby – you just have to give it the chance. Watch for the signals: when you see your baby needing to suck more often, make sure you give him the opportunity. Don't offer him a bottle or dummy instead, or you'll stop him from getting the message through to your breasts, and he'll be even more hungry tomorrow.

Talking about your feelings

Being with a small baby all day long is a wonderful privilege – there will be many occasions when you'll look down with love and pride at your growing child and reflect on how far you've come in so short a time.

But looking after a small baby on your own – as many women do – is tiring and sometimes lonely work. Babies are marvellous, but while you can chat to them all the time (and very good for them it is too!), they can't chat back about the book you're reading or the TV programme you watched last night. You do need other company sometimes, so if you're usually in the house on your own with the baby during the day, try to find like-minded friends to meet up with and chat to. Joining a pro-breastfeeding parenting organization can be an excellent way to do this, introducing you to people with useful experiences who you can turn to for support and advice.

Above all, don't soldier on alone. If you feel you've no energy, if getting up in the morning seems a huge hurdle or if you're finding it difficult to see the meaning or fun in life, you may have postnatal depression. Talk to someone – your partner, your mother or a health professional. If you are depressed, it may be difficult to get things into perspective, so do seek help.

MEETING NEW FRIENDS
It's useful to join groups or organizations to help find like-minded friends to chat to and who can offer you support and advice should you need it.

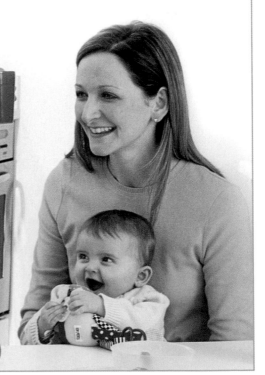

Fewer night feeds

Night-time feeds can be tiring, and cutting them down comes high on the wish list of most. You can help reduce the number of night-time feeds by:

● keeping the bedroom dark and interacting with your baby as little as possible when he wakes at night – this reinforces the message that night time is different from day, that it's when people are quiet and when they go to sleep rather than get up and play

● stroking his back or head rather than lifting him out of his cot when he wakes – he may fall off to sleep without a feed, which will help break the cycle of waking.

Is breastfeeding a contraceptive?

As you continue to breastfeed over the weeks and months after your baby's birth, your periods are unlikely to return. What this means is you almost certainly aren't ovulating, so you can't conceive another baby. It's important to realize that you shouldn't rely on breastfeeding as a contraceptive if you really don't want to conceive again straight away. But it seems to be the case that if:

● you have not had a period

● your baby is less than six months

● and you are breastfeeding exclusively, then you have only a two per cent chance of becoming pregnant.

It's nature's way of spacing babies – your body knows, as your breasts are making milk and feeding it frequently to your baby, that you've got your hands full and stops ovulation to give you a break from conceiving another child too soon.

Some women are happy to let nature take its course if they know they want another baby – what you need to know is that from the time your baby is six months old you are increasingly likely to become fertile again. However, some mothers who breastfeed do go

Troubleshooting

Hopefully you'll sail through breastfeeding without any problems. But just in case, here's what to do if:

● **you get sore nipples.**
Re-read the section in this book on positioning and latching on (see pages 14–15) because bad positioning is almost always the root cause of sore nipples. Talk to a lactation specialist so you can perfect your technique. Sometimes a simple suggestion will make all the difference. Expressing a little breast milk onto the sore nipple is a good way of relieving the pain.

● **you get one or more tender lumps in your breast.**
This may be a blocked duct. Feed your baby from this side as much as possible, have a warm bath, massage the firm area and express a little bit of milk while in the bath to get the milk moving through your breast again.

● **you start feeling feverish or have a red spot on your breast.**
This could be the start of mastitis or breast inflammation. Feed as much as possible from the affected breast, get lots of rest, move your arm on that side to help improve blood flow to the area. Go to your doctor for advice.

● **your baby has suddenly started to refuse his feeds.**
Your breast milk may have changed in flavour. Are you on medication? Have you been doing a lot of exercise, which can lead to a temporary build-up of lactic acid in your milk? Have your periods started again, or are you pregnant again? The hormonal changes could be making a difference. These changes to your breast milk are usually short-lived, and your baby soon starts to feed again. Another cause of a baby refusing to feed can be that he's got a blocked nose. If refusing feeds continues beyond two or three feeds, get medical help.

● **you think your baby is comfort sucking.**
If you think your baby is enjoying sucking at the breast, but isn't taking in a lot of milk, it may be that he is actually taking in more than you realize. Or he might be sucking to encourage your breasts to make more milk for tomorrow – upping the demand factor. Alternatively, he might just need to feel close to you right now – and who's to say that's not just as important as taking his milk?

for a year or even two without the resumption of their periods.

Most women, though, choose to exercise more control over their fertility. If you fall into this category, go to see a family planning specialist to discuss your needs – the method of birth control you've used in the past may no longer be the one best suited to your needs now.

Birth-control pills that contain oestrogen are likely to interfere with your milk supply, so the progesterone-only pill is more commonly prescribed, and no studies have shown there to be any harmful effect on the baby. Some mothers, despite this, choose not to take oral contraceptives while they're breastfeeding, and for them a barrier method (condoms or a diaphragm) may be the best option. If you decide to use a diaphragm or cap and have used one in the past, you must have a new one fitted now as childbirth changes the size of your cervix.

TEAM EFFORT
By giving his support and helping you while you breastfeed, your partner will quickly become part of the feeding routine.

INVOLVING SIBLINGS
Once you are breastfeeding confidently, talk to older siblings while you feed and try to make sure they don't feel left out.

Your partner's role

Will your partner feel left out because you're breastfeeding your baby? The answer to this is very complex: a mother and her breastfed baby have an extremely close and exclusive relationship and, inevitably, some dads do feel left out. But there are lots of ways in which your partner can support both you and your baby. In particular, he can spend time cuddling, and then playing with, his child; he can change his nappy and he can rock the crib.

Your partner can also help you get comfortable when you're starting a feed, and bring you a cup of water or tea if you need something to drink. He can help you recover from broken nights by taking the baby downstairs with him early in the morning, and he can make sure you eat nutritious meals by shopping for and cooking them.

No dad wants to feel as though he's been usurped by a newborn. Be sensitive to your partner's needs: like you, he's got a whole different way of life as a parent to get used to. Perhaps the biggest plus for both of you is that you have one another to share the delight of this new little person with.

Checklist

WHAT YOU NEED TO AVOID

- **Alcohol** Studies show that alcohol may be dangerous for the developing baby. Many women continue to abstain from alcohol while breastfeeding.

- **Smoking** This can reduce your milk supply. In addition, nicotine is passed on in breast milk. Thinking of your baby and his vulnerability to cigarette smoke could be a good tool in getting you to give up, and you should ask your family doctor for a referral to a therapist if you'd like to try. But if you carry on smoking don't think you can't breastfeed – your milk is still the best food for your baby, although you should always smoke away from him, preferably outside or at least in another room.

- **Drugs** If you need to take prescribed or over-the-counter drugs for any reason, always tell your health worker that you are breastfeeding.

- **Too much exercise** Heavy workouts can increase the amount of lactic acid in your milk, which may affect the taste of the milk, but for most mothers and babies this is not a problem.

- You should also avoid caffeine, too much spicy or acidic food, and peanuts if there is a history of peanut allergy in the family.

Can I breastfeed while I'm out and about?

It's normal to feel a bit apprehensive and self-conscious when you first breastfeed in public. What you'll find, though, is that the more you do it, the easier it gets. And it's worth getting used to breastfeeding out and about because doing so means you'll maximize the benefits – after all, breast milk is the best convenience food ever invented!

Tips for breastfeeding in public

Get confident about breastfeeding before you do it in front of other people or in a public place – it can be daunting at first, so try to make it as easy and straightforward as possible. Have someone with you – ideally, another breastfeeding mother.

★ Choose a place where there are other parents and small children, so you'll feel among friends.

★ Take a change of clothes for you and your baby.

★ Breastfeeding can make you thirsty, so always carry a bottle of water for yourself in your bag.

★ Wear a cardigan or jacket over your top – if your breasts leak you'll be able to cover it up.

★ If your milk lets down when you aren't ready to feed, press hard on your breasts with your upper arms – this inhibits the flow.

Breastfeeding rooms

Some shops and shopping centres have breastfeeding rooms where mothers can take their babies to feed them "discreetly". Many breastfeeding mothers don't like the idea of being shut away in a little room –

they say no one should be made to feel they have to hide themselves away to breastfeed. Others feel that they can't breastfeed publicly and, for them, breastfeeding rooms make the difference between being able to go out and having to stay at home.

Baby comes first

Wherever you are and whoever you are with, if your baby needs a breastfeed that should come first and those around you should respect that.

If for any reason you feel uncomfortable, simply excuse yourself and find somewhere you prefer to sit. Remember that the more breastfeeding mothers choose to feed their babies out and about, the more accepted and "normal" this will be.

It's also important to know that breastfeeding can be discreet – often those sitting around you won't notice you doing it, especially as you become more adept at it. And as a breastfeeding mother you've usually got the law on your side if you choose to feed your baby in public. Many people will show support for you if they do notice you're feeding your baby: if you attract any attention at all, it's more likely to be positive than negative.

EASY DISCRETION
Pulling a top up from the waist to breastfeed in public will attract less attention than unbuttoning a shirt. It's also a good idea to carry a light shawl with you in case you feel the need for extra cover.

CAREFUL POSITIONING
If you're in a café or restaurant, choose a seat facing away from other customers – this will make you feel less self-conscious as you feed. More than likely, those sitting around you won't even notice you doing it.

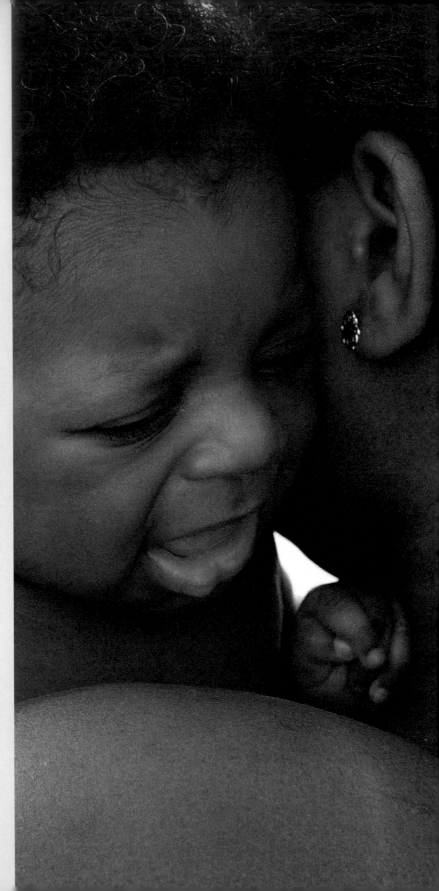

" I can feel my heartbeat quickening when I hear Alexa crying. It really does **trigger** a strong reaction. I need to respond to her and find ways of **calming her down.** "

GINA, mother of nine-month-old Alexa

Crying in young babies

Imagine for a moment what life might be like if your baby never cried. You would have no way of knowing that he was hungry, ill or in pain, or simply needed a hug. Crying is an important part of your baby's survival mechanism. It's a signal that is virtually impossible for parents to ignore, and a highly effective way of ensuring that you will quickly respond to his needs, whatever they happen to be.

The significance of crying

Your baby's cry is designed to grab your attention. On hearing it, your body produces stress hormones that increase your blood pressure and heart rate and tense your muscles. You are very keen to solve the crying.

Crying also promotes "attachment" – the way in which you bond with your baby when love grows between you. It does this by ensuring that you keep your baby close to you and provide him with plenty of loving attention. Indeed, research has found that babies who have formed a poor emotional attachment to their parents may sometimes cry inconsolably to get the attention they desperately need.

To begin with, crying is also your baby's main "language" for expressing his needs. Then, as other ways of communicating (especially speech) develop, you will notice that your baby cries less because he doesn't need to rely on crying as a way of making himself understood. Having said that, he will continue to cry throughout childhood, and adulthood, to signal distress.

Patterns and peaks

Your baby cries most during the first three months, after which the rate of crying tends to drop to about half its earlier level. Some babies naturally cry more than others, and there is evidence that these *relative* amounts of crying remain up to one year of age. This means that babies who cry more than others in the first three months are likely to still be crying more until the age of one, even though they are crying less than they were. Perhaps surprisingly, your baby's level of

How long do babies cry?

Most babies who grow up in Western societies cry on average for approximately:

- two hours a day in the first three months

- one hour a day in the four-to-12-months period.

Remember, these are *average* figures. Many babies cry more than this, so don't worry if yours is one of them. Interestingly, studies of non-Western communities, in which there is more frequent body contact and demand feeding, suggest that babies there seem to cry less.

Questions & Answers

My three-month-old baby can be very happy, gurgling at her mobile or listening to music one minute, then quite suddenly she starts screaming and goes into a meltdown. Why is this?
It is likely that your baby is showing you that she has become over-stimulated. When this happens, move her to a more peaceful area away from too many toys, sights and sounds. You can try to spot this coming from her body language – she may turn her head away or squeeze her eyes shut, for example, before the crying frenzy starts.

crying is not at its highest when he is a newborn. The rate of crying gradually increases from birth until a baby is around six weeks old, then it subsides. This is often referred to as the developmental crying peak.

In the first three months, evening crying makes up about 40 per cent of the daily total, and about half of all parents report an evening crying peak – usually early evening (see pages 42–45).

Between the ages of about nine and 12 months, night-time crying becomes more common, although again this is often a pattern shown by babies who have been excessive criers up until then.

Coping with change

There is considerable recent evidence to show that a lot of what causes your baby to cry during the first few months is simply developmental. From birth, your baby has to go

THE FIRST CRY
Your baby's first cry announces that he is taking his first breaths, and is missing the security of the womb.

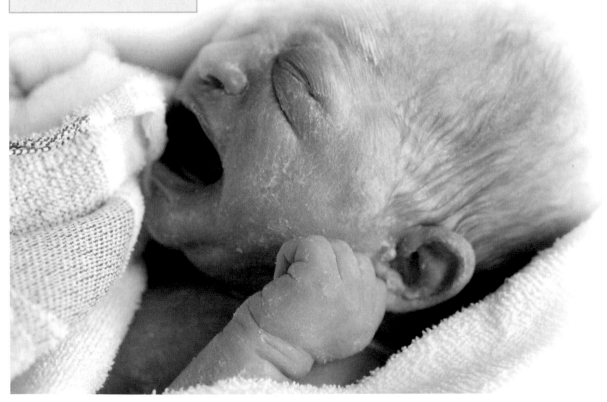

Sensitive babies

Some babies can be shown to have a low sensory threshold – in other words they are more sensitive than other babies. They seem to miss the safety of the womb and are readily overwhelmed by new experiences. You can probably recognize this if your baby is one who dislikes being bathed or undressed. Typically, sensitive babies tend to:

- change more rapidly from one behaviour state to another, for example from sleeping to crying
- be easily startled more often
- more frequently tense or jerk their arms and legs.

Sensitive babies may cry as a result of food passing down through their digestive system, having wind, and even from the physical feelings of their own bodies, such as the movement of their arms and legs.

External sensations may be too much for these babies. Sounds, light, smells or faces suddenly coming too close to them, even being picked up and held, especially by a number of different people, can be upsetting.

If you recognize your baby as being of a sensitive nature, he will enjoy calm, peaceful surroundings and careful handling.

Checklist

To help interpret your baby's needs, think of his crying as a graded signal, the level of which represents increasing distress.

- **Intensity** Consider how loud the crying is. Does the intensity decrease when you hold your baby?

- **Constancy** Note how long your baby's crying lasts. Does it stop when you hold him?

- **Pattern** Note also when the crying occurs. Is it mainly in the morning, afternoon, evening or night? Before, during or after feeds? Is it every day, or more on weekdays than at the weekend? Is it when he's missed a nap, after being handled a lot or being in a stimulating environment?

- **Length of crying** How many hours a day does your baby's crying last, on average?

through huge changes, physically, socially and psychologically. It's normal for a baby to have bouts of more persistent crying before a particular developmental stage. It may be connected to major changes in the baby's brain and nervous system when a new developmental challenge is met.

This means that all babies will cry a certain amount, no matter what you do to try to soothe them. So it is not always helpful to think that "something's wrong" or to wear yourself out trying to find solutions to stop the crying.

Excessive crying

Excessive crying is defined as more than three hours' crying in a 24-hour period. As many as one in four babies, from newborn to three months of age, display this level of crying. Many theories of why babies cry excessively have been tested by researchers but have proven to be unfounded. These include over-feeding or under-feeding, trapped wind, "colic" (see pages 42–45), the mother's age, the sex of the baby, allergies, the parents' IQ or educational level, whether they are first-time parents, spoiling, and even whether the baby's mother smoked or drank coffee in pregnancy.

Your baby's temperament

Some babies are more "challenging" than others, and it is simply in their temperament to cry more. It is worth considering that your baby may need a very high level of care and closeness for a while to aid his development, and that crying is a vital, if rather exaggerated, way to ensure he gets the necessary attention. Even if you have a challenging baby, remember that:

● your baby's crying is *never* his "fault"

● it's certainly not your fault, either

● it does not mean that your child will grow up to be difficult or bad-tempered.

There is no evidence that excessive crying has any effect on development or behaviour beyond the first year. He *will* grow out of this stage.

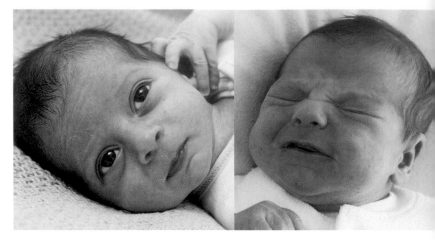

WHAT'S HIS TEMPERAMENT?
He may be active, sensitive, easily over-stimulated or a bit of everything. Getting to know him will help you comfort him.

Sensing your tension

It has been suggested that a baby can pick up on a parent's tension. You may find that even though you try your best to soothe your crying baby, someone else – your partner, health visitor or a friend – can calm him down more easily.

As a new mother, you may find this very disheartening. You may even start to think that your baby doesn't like you. It is only too easy to feel rejected when your baby seems to dislike being held, or thrashes around crying when you try to carry him in a sling.

While it is tempting to think that you must be doing something wrong, the likelihood is that you are feeling so upset by the crying because of your strong emotional bond with your baby, you become tense and irritable. Your baby senses this build-up of tension in you and cries all the more. So a vicious circle begins. Make the most of others' offers of help – and if they can soothe your baby in the process, so much the better!

What those cries could mean

Research may not support the theory that a baby's cries sound different depending on his needs, but many parents believe that they can identify several types of crying from their babies – for example, hunger, pain or irritability – and this helps them try to find ways to soothe them.

● **Hunger** In the early days, hunger is most likely to be the main reason for your baby's cries. It is the most obvious, and easiest to deal with. A hunger cry is very persistent and is unlikely to stop until your baby is fed.

● **The need for attention** A baby who needs your attention and probably wants a cuddle may sound "grizzly".

● **Pain or fright** If your baby is in pain or has been startled by something, his cries are likely to be a very sharp yell.

● **Illness** Although this is rarely the reason that he's crying, an ill baby's cry may be unusual in some way – higher-pitched, for example.

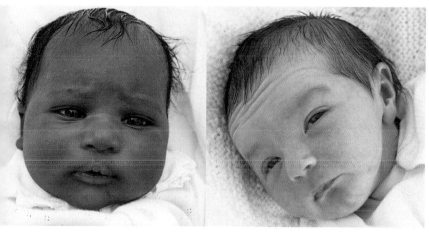

" No matter what is causing Joseph's crying, he loves being held up against my shoulder while I rub his back. "

CHRISTINA is mum to nine-week-old Joseph

Questions & Answers

I had a long and difficult labour, and eventually a forceps delivery. My son is five weeks old now and seems hard to settle. Has his birth experience had anything to do with it?

It's true that some babies may cry more following a complicated delivery or obstetric interventions, such as a forceps, ventouse or Caesarean birth.

Also, babies who have been born prematurely, or who have spent time in special care, may cry more and need especially sensitive care. It could be that they are experiencing more discomfort or pain, or it may just be that they are finding it harder to cope with all the normal sights and sounds because of their immaturity.

Consider also the effect the birth may have had on you. A negative birth experience can lead to mothers taking less pleasure in their babies, who may then cry more. A baby who is difficult to console can in turn increase a mother's feelings of inadequacy, which makes the situation worse. Talk this through with your doctor, who can offer advice and check that your baby is well.

Emotional discomfort

All babies need the comfort and reassurance of being held close as often as possible in the early days. If you have ruled out all the potential physical causes of your baby's crying (see below, right), she probably needs soothing.

● **Insecurity** Your baby may settle quite happily in your arms or a sling, then be fretful when put down. This is a clear sign that she wants to be near you.

● **Boredom** As your baby gets older, from around five months,

she could be crying because she is bored and wants something – or someone – to amuse her. This could happen sooner if she's an active, wakeful baby.

● **Over-stimulation** Too much handling, noise, even play, can make your baby irritable and fretful.

● **Overtiredness** An overtired baby needs calm handling. To help relax her and soothe her so that she's able to go to sleep, try gentle rocking, singing, cuddling, stroking or sitting with her in a quiet, darkened room.

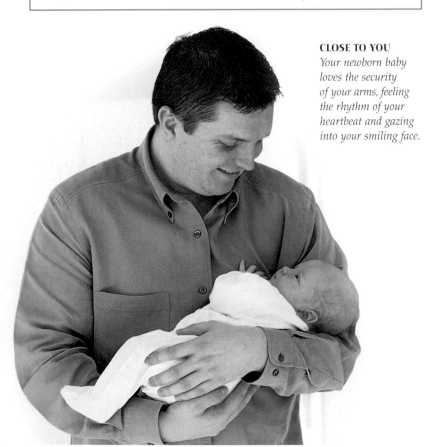

CLOSE TO YOU
Your newborn baby loves the security of your arms, feeling the rhythm of your heartbeat and gazing into your smiling face.

Adjusting to the world

Newborn babies must make a big adjustment in the first few days of life outside the womb. For some babies, the shock to their senses caused by this arrival is probably just too much, and they express their feelings of discomfort by crying vigorously due to the many unfamiliar sensations of light, noise and sometimes even the touch of many different people. In the early weeks, a lot of your baby's crying probably happens simply because you have not yet learned what she likes and dislikes. This takes time and paying attention to all your baby's verbal and behavioural

Physical discomfort

There are many physical reasons why your baby could be crying.

● **Hunger** As soon as your baby feels hungry, she will cry to be fed. Before she starts to cry, look for early hunger signs, such as rooting, sucking and even opening and closing her hands over her chest.

● **Thirst** Newborn babies usually do not need extra fluids, other than their normal feeds. If your baby appears thirsty, try offering a little more.

● **A dirty or wet nappy** While needing a nappy change may not

communication cues. Spend time observing your baby to help you to get to know her and understand her needs. Try not to compare her with other babies.

It's important to remember that:
- some babies prefer quiet, still times and very gentle handling, while others want more activity and may seem desperate to grow up
- some take heartily to feeding; others find it a struggle for a while
- some can be put down easily to settle after feeding; others will always complain and cry
- some babies may need to cry more to ensure that their higher demands for contact and care are met – a reminder that crying is also an attachment-promoting behaviour.

If your baby does seem to cry a lot, it is even more important to make the most of times when she is content to observe, and interact with her. This will increase the bond between you.

Your personality

If you are a naturally calm person, you may be better able to cope with crying than a more stressed parent would be. This is why individual parents' interpretations of crying vary – one may describe as excessive and unbearable crying that another finds challenging but possible to cope with.

Your home life

Your personal circumstances will also have an impact on how easy it is for you to manage a crying baby. If you have the support of a partner, perhaps the experience of having had other children, or friends or family who can share the load with you, then you will probably manage more easily than a single or first-time mother with few friends or relatives living nearby.

If you are on your own, find out about mother-and-baby groups in your area – you will find the friendship and support you receive from meeting other mums an invaluable lifeline.

make every baby cry, leaving your baby in a wet or soiled nappy can aggravate her delicate skin.

- **Wind** Trapped wind can be uncomfortable. Keep her as upright as possible during a feed, and "wind" her by holding her against your shoulder and rubbing or patting her back.

- **Feeling too hot or too cold** Young babies are not able to regulate their own temperature and need your help to make them feel comfortable. To check whether your baby is too hot (or too cold), feel her tummy not her hands or feet. Take off (or add) extra layers accordingly. Remove extra clothing from her when you enter a warm environment, even if she is asleep.

- **Needing a change of position** Before she can shift her position by herself, your baby may cry for help if she is lying uncomfortably. Remember, however, that you must always lay her down to sleep on her back to avoid the risk of Sudden Infant Death Syndrome (SIDS).

How can I comfort my newborn baby?

As you react to your baby's cry, your first thoughts are, "Why is she crying?" and, "How can I soothe her?" If there's no obvious physical cause for her crying (see page 33), she'll need your help to calm down. Find out which comforting method works best for your baby and repeat it systematically. If one thing doesn't work, try several together – it's a question of trial and error.

Cuddles, contact and bonding

★ Rocking in your arms Research has shown that your heartbeat, rhythmical breathing pattern and regular movements help to establish a baby's own regular heart rate, respiratory and sleep patterns. You may find you instinctively sway your hips whenever you hold your baby close.

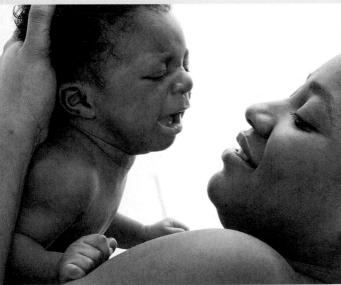

A DIFFERENT APPROACH
Don't worry if a tried-and-trusted method of soothing your baby seems not to work. It's worth persevering with other ways of comforting her until you find one that she can't resist.

TENDER LOVING CARE
Your warm embrace will usually prove to be irresistible to your newborn, helping her feel secure, loved and confident that you are there to meet her needs.

FEELING BETTER
As you rock her in your arms or hold her against your shoulder, watch for signs that her crying is subsiding and that she's ready to drop off to sleep.

★ **A sling** Carrying your baby in a sling can give comfort and closeness, as well as providing movement for her. It also leaves your hands free.

★ **Stroking** Gentle stroking of the forehead, or anywhere on your baby's body, may help her relax.

★ **Massage** This is the perfect way to soothe and bond with your baby (see pages 40–41). Soft stroking and massage are easy to do and both you and your baby will benefit from the intimacy.

Other ways to comfort

★ **Sounds and music** Anything from lullabies to pop songs can help. Also try recordings of womb sounds, or "white noise", the monotonous hum of the washing machine or vacuum cleaner.

★ **Going for a ride** You may rock your baby when she's in her pram or cradle and discover that she quietens because of the movement. Taking her out for a walk in her pram or pushchair, or a ride in the car, may also be effective for this reason. However, make sure that your baby doesn't come to rely on this as a way of getting to sleep – she needs to learn to do this by herself.

Expert tips

The following are causes for crying related to feeding.

● If she's crying during a feed, check that your baby is latched on properly. Her mouth should take in a large part of your areola, not just the nipple, and her lower lip should be turned out. Ask your midwife or partner to check.

● Make sure your baby's nose is clear of your breast so that she can breathe.

● If you have a full breast, your milk may gush out too quickly at the start of a feed and choke and upset your baby. Try expressing some milk first.

● If your baby still seems hungry after a breastfeed, offer her more. If you are bottle-feeding, ask your health visitor for advice before increasing your baby's feeds.

● If bottle-feeding, check that you are using the correct size of teat for the age of your baby. If the hole is too large, the milk will come out too fast and make your baby choke. If it is too small, the milk will flow too slowly, frustrating your baby. Use the same type of teat for each feed so that your baby learns to adjust to the flow.

● Your baby will take more milk when she has a growth spurt, often at around six weeks and again at 12 to 14 weeks. It can take a few days for your breasts to catch up to meet this demand and she may cry more until the right supply is established.

● If your baby cries regularly after a feed, try winding her (see page 33).

Feeding and crying

In the early weeks, it is normal for your baby to want to feed frequently – every two hours is not unusual. Small pre-term babies may need to feed even more often than this to catch up with their growing. Often they are awake more at night and want to sleep all day.

There are several reasons why your newborn needs frequent feeds.

● Breast milk is perfect food for your newborn, but it is low in fat and protein, so she digests it quickly and easily and is soon hungry again.

● Your newborn has a tiny stomach, so "little and often" is best for her.

● It takes time for both you and your baby to learn how to breastfeed efficiently.

● Remember also that breastfeeding works on a "supply-and-demand" basis, so that as your baby sucks, your breasts are stimulated into

❞ We both get so much out of breastfeeding. It helps me relax, and I know I'm giving him the best possible start. ❞

MELISSA is mum to 12-week-old Daniel

making more milk for the next feed. To keep up with demand, ensure that you eat a nutritious diet, and drink plenty of fluids. This is especially important when you feel you need to increase your milk supply.

● Trying to feed your newborn baby by the clock will inevitably lead to a lot more crying as it takes several weeks for her feeding to settle into a routine.

Sleeping and crying

In the beginning, your baby doesn't really know the difference between night and day, and it is better to accept your baby's rhythms and routines for now. Trying to fit your baby into an imaginary schedule at this stage will lead to more crying.

Helping your baby

After the first few months, however, it is worth thinking about sleep routines, and you can begin to set up bedtime rituals, such as a bath, a cuddle and a story, in the evening. These are signals that even tiny babies start to recognize.

Even for daytime naps, by about four months it is worth putting your baby down at set times, and in a recognizable way if you can, preferably in the cot in her bedroom.

Sleep facts

It is important to remember that:

● a baby's internal body clock is not fully developed until at least six weeks

● babies' sleep patterns are quite different from those of adults. They spend much longer in light, active REM (rapid-eye-movement) sleep, when they are more likely to wake – 50 per cent of the time compared with 25 per cent in adults

● premature babies spend even more time in light sleep

● it is not until six months or more that a baby's brain regulates sleep in a similar way to an adult's.

The benefits of swaddling

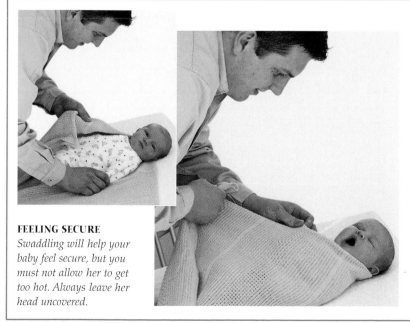

FEELING SECURE
Swaddling will help your baby feel secure, but you must not allow her to get too hot. Always leave her head uncovered.

Wrapping your newborn quite firmly, "papoose style", in a light blanket or sheet could help to calm her, especially if she's sensitive and easily startled. Many babies are upset by the jerking movements of their limbs, and swaddling prevents this happening.

Fold the blanket or sheet and lay your baby on top of it. Her neck should be level with the fold. Bring one side of the blanket over her body and tuck it firmly under her. Then do the same with the other side. Tuck the end of the blanket under her feet and legs. You may wrap her arms, or leave them free so that she can get her hands to her mouth to soothe herself.

Checklist

When it feels as though your young baby's crying is getting on top of you, take a break (see pages 46–47). The following facts may help you to put things into perspective.

- It is not possible to spoil a baby by going to her when she cries.

- Your newborn is never just "exercising her lungs".

- Her crying is a reflex to express needs or to get help when she can't cope alone with the overwhelming changes in her world.

- Your newborn never cries to manipulate you. She is using the only language she has at the beginning to ensure that her needs are met.

Meeting her needs – fast!

There is a great deal of evidence that the more quickly you can meet your baby's cries in the early days, by going immediately to respond to her, the more you will be helping to build a feeling of security and confidence. As a result, your baby is less likely to cry excessively later on. There is also a developmental reason for not leaving your newborn to cry for too long.

Being loving and responsive in the early days can actually help your baby's brain develop, and lead to better language development. Having said that, many babies fuss or cry for a short time when first put down, so you may need to leave her for a few minutes to settle – but never more than five minutes for a new baby.

Take a realistic view

It helps if you can have a realistic view of what having a baby is really like. This can be difficult when we see everywhere images of perfectly contented, smiling babies, being cared for by parents who appear to be totally relaxed and confident in their role. Some parents may have had no chance to learn that the reality may sometimes be like that, but there will also be many challenges to face.

The attitude of others may not help the assumptions that a "good" baby doesn't cry, and a "good" parent can always solve crying. Neither of these things is true.

If you are becoming very upset by your new baby's crying, someone less emotionally involved, such as your partner, may be able to soothe her more easily. Remember that this is not a reflection on you – your baby's behaviour is not related to you being a bad mother, nor is it because she doesn't like you. She can react to your tension, so you must share the care and find ways to relax.

Involving dads

Research shows lots of benefits when dads are fully involved with the day-to-day care of their babies. Their emotional support in the early days is vital, and will make a big difference to you, especially while you are getting breastfeeding established successfully.

Your partner can also play a key role in the early emotional development of your baby. He will create loving bonds by carrying out all the same physical and emotional care that you do.

It's also important that you involve your partner right from the beginning. Not only will his help give you a break, it also prevents him feeling that he's missing out on caring for your baby or that you are so involved with her, you no longer have any time left over for him.

Even if you are breastfeeding your baby, there are many other ways your partner can get involved. He can still cuddle, "wind" and bath her, and change nappies and comfort her when she's crying. He can carry her in a sling, and take her out for a walk in the pram or pushchair. Dads are just as capable of doing all the practical babycare activities as mums, and can be equally hands-on parents. The more opportunities they have to hold and cuddle their babies, the more confident and relaxed they become, and the closer their bond. Everyone gains from it.

SOFT AND GENTLE
Your newborn is likely to be soothed by the soft feel of a fleece against her delicate skin. But be careful not to let her sleep on a fleece because of the risk of suffocation.

Self-comforting

Sucking is the most obvious source of comfort for all crying babies. Your newborn can suck the breast, bottle or a dummy, or you can help her to try to find her own fist or your clean fingers. Although it is well known that babies suck their thumbs in the womb, it will be two or three months before they really learn to suck their thumbs effectively.

Can massage help ease my baby's crying?

Baby massage can be relaxing and beneficial for both babies and parents. Through eye contact and touch, it promotes bonding and boosts your baby's confidence and wellbeing. There is even evidence that it can reduce crying levels and relieve "colic", encourage better sleep patterns and possibly help boost your baby's immune system. Massage is generally recommended for healthy full-term babies. It is better not to massage your baby if she seems ill or has had a recent immunization. Baby massage classes are an ideal way to learn the techniques – and to make new friends. Your health visitor should have information.

Massaging tips

★ You can massage your baby when she's undressed or through her clothes.

★ Make sure that the room is warm.

★ Your hands should be clean and warm. You may like to use baby oil (avoid aromatherapy and nut-based oils).

★ Pay attention to your baby's cues that she is enjoying the massage. Some babies find it stimulating; others like only one part of their body massaged.

★ Massage is best in between feeds, not just after or just before one.

HER HEAD AND SHOULDERS
Using the tips of your fingers or thumb, gently stroke your baby's forehead out to her temple, then her neck to her shoulders. If she's alert, keep eye contact, talk softly and smile at her.

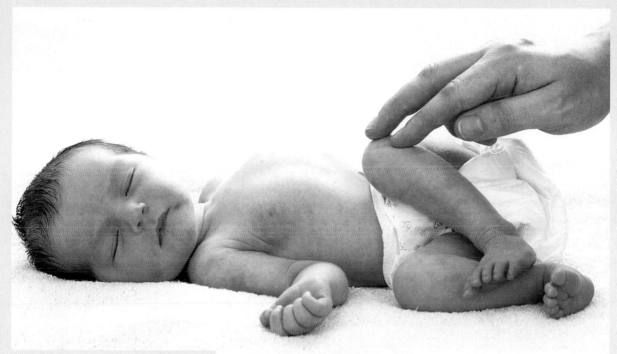

HER LEGS

Making small circular strokes with your fingertips, or gently squeezing with your hand, massage down from her thighs to her knees, and then down her shins to her ankles. You could work one leg at a time or both simultaneously.

HER HANDS AND ARMS

From her shoulders, continue your strokes down along her arm to her hand. Again, you could work on one limb at a time or both together. Next, try some very gentle circular strokes on her tummy, using one hand.

HER FEET

Working down her legs, massage her ankles, her feet and finally each of her toes. You could finish by gently cycling her legs.

Excessive crying

Also know as "colic", this is a distressing pattern of crying that is at the end of the spectrum of normal crying, and is something babies "do", rather than something they "have". Colic is not an "illness" in itself, and in the vast majority of cases there is no underlying medical cause. Having said that, it is important that you consult your doctor if you are at all worried about your baby, so that he can rule out any health problems and reassure you that your baby is well.

Unexplained, and often inconsolable, crying is unusual in that it does not fit well with the idea that babies cry in order to have a need met. You may try everything, and yet your baby still cries.

In fact, it has been shown that, despite crying excessively, babies do not have the body changes that might be expected. Their heart rates

COMFORTING HOLD
A baby with colic may be soothed by being held in a position that allows gentle pressure on her abdomen.

What are the causes?

There have been many unproven theories in the past over what might be the cause of colic, from food intolerances and parental tension, to trapped wind, and evening hunger in breastfed babies. The current thinking about colic crying gives the following possible explanations:

• your baby may have an immature nervous system, especially if she seems very reactive to external factors – lights, sounds or activities going on around her

• she may be a sensitive baby, needing to cry to block out other distressing sensations

• crying at the end of the day may be your baby's way of releasing tension

• she is having difficulty regulating her behaviour and once she starts crying she doesn't know how to stop – she needs your help to settle (see pages 44–45)

• it's all down to your baby's temperament – some babies simply cry more than others.

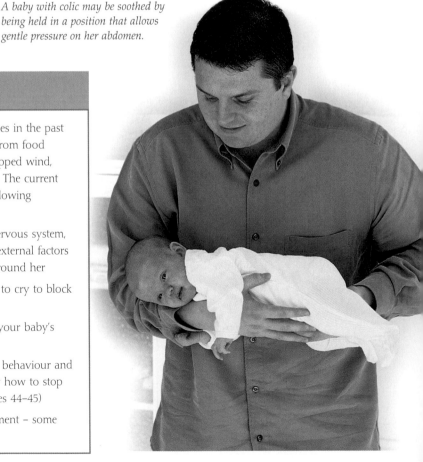

" Scott has just turned three months old and his colic is completely gone. He is much more cheerful, and easier to settle. We can relax in the evenings now! "

GEMMA is mum to three-month-old Scott

and levels of cortisol – a chemical in the blood that is an indicator of stress – may remain within the normal range, even when crying their hardest!

This type of crying could even be considered to be a lot like sleep difficulties, in that it is a problem, *but not for your baby*. It is the effect these behaviours have on you, her parents, that is the real issue.

Medical concerns

In the past, it has been suggested that colic could be the result of a problem with a baby's immature central nervous or gastrointestinal system. Feeding difficulties, or a dietary intolerance of some kind, perhaps to cows' milk protein, have also been put forward as possible causes.

Recent research has concluded, however, that it would be in only a small minority, possibly about 10 per cent of cases, that digestive problems could cause this extreme form of crying. Yet, parents are often told, as the first response, to change their method of feeding.

However, colic occurs more or less equally in bottle-fed and breastfed babies, so realistically, any change would have an effect on only a small number of colicky babies.

Waiting it out

Hang on to the fact that *all* crying settles down after three or four months. Even though babies who are excessive criers may cry more than other babies until at least five months, they will be crying much less than before.

A colicky baby will not become a more difficult toddler or child.

How can I comfort my baby with colic?

Even though you try your best to keep a positive attitude throughout your baby's extreme crying bouts and fervently hold on to the fact that it will end in a few weeks, you probably feel happier trying something – anything! – to comfort your baby, if only for a short while.

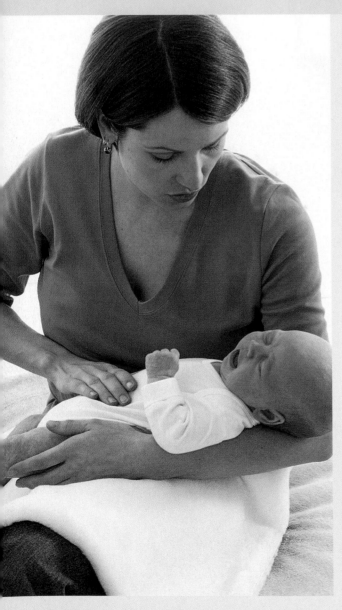

Physical contact

Remember, babies who have more physical contact may cry less. The benefits of cuddles and stroking have a well-proven physiological basis, and even when your baby's crying is not soothed, you may be boosting her immune system and growth hormones. Physical contact is always worthwhile.

It's also worth trying all the usual comfort tips for crying, such as sucking, rocking, playing music or singing, and massage (see pages 40–41). They may help for a while – but don't be surprised if, after a brief lull, your baby starts crying again. Find the three to five most successful strategies and rotate them through in the same order.

Soothing techniques

Other comforting tips to consider trying include:
★ doing a "colic dance", in which you rock your baby up and down while swaying your hips from side to side

GENTLE PRESSURE ON HER TUMMY
Holding your baby in the crook of your arm, place your hand on your baby's tummy and rub it gently. At the same time, maintain eye contact and talk to her softly, using her name regularly.

★ applying gentle pressure to your baby's tummy and rubbing gently

★ holding your baby in positions that allow pressure on her abdomen, for example over your knees, across the crook of your arm or upright against your shoulder

★ applying warmth to your baby's tummy, such as the gentle heat from a covered hot water bottle filled with warm – not hot – water held against her through her clothes

★ giving her a bath – but do be sensitive to your baby's temperament. Some colicky babies find a bath soothing, while others are more agitated by it

★ winding your baby – try keeping her as upright as possible during feeds, or break off from a feed, hold her against your shoulder and gently rub her back to help her to bring the wind up

★ using homeopathic remedies, such as colocynthis, or herbal drinks, such as fennel or chamomile. *Always* consult a qualified practitioner who specializes in treating babies and children before giving any complementary remedies

★ trying cranial osteopathy (see page 49), which may help if your baby has misaligned skull bones following birth. Again, always use a qualified practitioner.

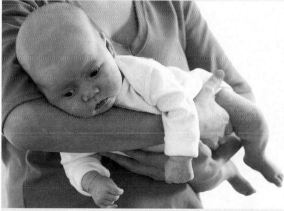

FACE DOWN
Holding your baby in the crook of your arm allows you to apply gentle pressure to her tummy, while swaying her from side to side. She'll feel secure as her body is supported along the length of your arm, and the movement may also distract and soothe her.

PAT HER BACK
When you feel confident with this position, and have a secure hold on the thigh of her leg furthest from your body, use your free hand to pat gently or rub her back using circular movements.

Checklist

Help your other children by:

• encouraging them to talk about their feelings

• sympathizing with them about how distracting the crying can be, reassuring them that this period will not last very long, and that soon you will have more time for them again

• thinking of ways to give them undivided attention. Perhaps your partner could play with your toddler more, or you could settle down to read to her while you feed the baby

• involving your children as much as possible in helping to amuse or calm the baby. Turn it into a family project!

• taking up all offers of help. Going to the cinema with a grandparent or a sleepover with a friend will be a welcome treat for older children.

" My older children have been so helpful, which is good because I find the more time I can spend comforting Orin, the more relaxed we all are. "

FRAN is mum to two-week-old Orin

A baby in the family

As your family grows, you may find yourself with a baby, a demanding toddler and a child just starting school. You now have a diverse set of relationships to manage, as well as your baby's crying. You may have to explore a range of solutions in order to keep going some of the essential activities of your normal family routine. It is important for all of you to hang on to the fact that these changes in family dynamics are to be expected for a while, and that things will soon return to normal.

When a baby arrives, it's a time of very mixed emotions. Younger children may be quite upset by the idea that the baby may be feeling sad. Older children may find that it interferes with their routines and feel that they are missing out on a good

Getting help

Never be afraid to ask for help, and take up all offers from your partner, grandparents, other family members or friends.

- Talk to other parents – they have all been there! Find out if there are any postnatal groups you can join in your area.

- Talk to your healthcare professional for general advice and support – particularly if you feel you're beginning to find it hard to cope (see page 48).

- Look on the Internet for parent support groups, or see *Useful Contacts* on pages 156–157.

deal of their parents' attention. All siblings may be annoyed or even angry at the many challenges a new baby brings. But then they are also likely to feel guilty about or be unable to understand these negative thoughts.

Be positive

You will inevitably have some guilty moments over how your older children's lives have changed with the arrival of a new baby, and feel yourself pulled in all directions. But don't allow guilt to take away the time your baby needs from you to feel secure. Always remember that

your baby's crying is not your fault, and it is not a reflection on your abilities as a parent either.

Be confident

Try to feel confident enough to ignore unhelpful advice about how other people manage crying, when the tone and implication are that you are getting it wrong.

The best type of help you need at the moment is from someone who can provide practical support, giving you a break by taking the baby for a while, or emotional support as a non-judgemental listening ear.

Expert tips

- Be as honest as you can about how the baby's crying is making everybody feel. It can be hard to express negative thoughts, because the social pressures are so great to pretend that everything is perfect when a new baby arrives. But it can really help everybody to feel relieved that these thoughts and feelings are normal and will pass.

- Consider separate beds or bedrooms for a while so that you and your partner each have the much-needed chance to catch up on sleep and rest. Take turns spending nights with the baby – obviously you won't have this option if you are breastfeeding, unless you express some milk, but even a few hours' unbroken sleep can be restful.

- Talk things through with your family, and draw up lists of what absolutely needs to be done, and who can do what. Older children may surprise you with their sensible suggestions and offers of help.

- Ask older children to help you keep a diary of your baby's crying (see page 48) – they will feel important to be given the task, and you may all be amazed to find that the crying lasts for less time than you thought.

- Keep your sense of humour – just pulling a funny face and saying to your toddler, "Oh no, here we go again!" when the baby starts to cry may lighten everybody's mood.

Expert tips

Help your baby or child feel comfortable when she's ill.

● If your baby has a fever, take her temperature and consult your doctor if it is over 38°C (100.4°F). Give liquid paracetamol suitable for children according to your doctor's instructions.

● To make her feel more comfortable, and to try to reduce the fever, keep her room cool and dress her in lightweight cotton clothing.

● Give her plenty of fluids to drink, to avoid dehydration.

● Keep an eye on your baby, even when she's asleep. Put her down where you can see her.

The crying paradox

In one way, nature seems to have slipped up. Crying is obviously meant to elicit the care needed for survival, ensuring loving interaction and adequate nutrition from parents. Yet, when it goes on and on, it can become "aversive". Studies have shown that some parents feel angry and less sympathetic towards a baby who cries excessively. If you are experiencing this, you will be feeling vulnerable, and you need help and support now. Don't feel guilty – no one has infinite patience. Recognizing that you need help is a positive step, so consult your doctor, or call Cry-sis (see page 156).

Seeking medical advice

Much research has shown that illness is a cause for crying in only a very small percentage of cases. Nevertheless, it is worth consulting your doctor, who can check that there are no underlying medical conditions or health problems, and reassure you that your baby is well.

It will help you, and your doctor, to keep a diary of your baby's crying for a week or two. Armed with this information, your doctor will be better able to understand your concerns. Your diary should make note of:

● the average number of hours your baby cries per day
● the number of days a week that her crying is a problem
● the intensity of the crying
● the constancy of the crying
● the pattern of the crying throughout the day (e.g. after a feed)
● anything that seems to make the crying better or worse.

Minor conditions

There are a number of minor conditions that may cause your baby to cry and, again, your doctor, health visitor or pharmacist will be able to advise you on the best course of action to take to help her.

KEEPING A CRYING DIARY
A diary is a useful record for your doctor, as well as a way of reassuring you that your baby's crying may not be as persistent as it seems!

● **Colds and coughs** A blocked nose may cause your baby to cry from frustration when feeding as she won't be able to breathe properly. Also, stuffiness and an irritating cough may keep her awake at night, making her overtired, and leading to crying. Ask your pharmacist to recommend an over-the-counter treatment.

● **Nappy rash** Feeling sore means that urine may sting and cause your baby to cry every time she wets her nappy. Change her nappy frequently, letting the air get to her skin, and use a barrier cream to protect her.

● **Thrush** Oral thrush is a fungal infection that can make feeding painful. Look for white patches inside her mouth, which will not come off if you gently wipe them with a clean handkerchief. Your doctor may prescribe medication.

- **Teething** Once your baby starts cutting her teeth, she may experience some discomfort until the tooth breaks through her gum.

- **Urinary tract infection** This can be hard to spot in babies, although there may be a fever as well as more crying than usual. An older child may pass urine more often, and it may be cloudy or smelly. Your doctor will test the urine and prescribe antibiotics.

Complementary therapies

Complementary therapies are sometimes used by parents looking to lessen their babies' crying. Massage is used to boost a baby's wellbeing and promote relaxation and bonding, while homeopathy can help with digestive problems. Cranial osteopathy is used to improve persistent crying and to calm restless babies. It is based on the theory that cranial faults can develop when the bones of a baby's skull are compressed during birth. Very gentle manipulation is used to move them into the correct position.

Before visiting any complementary practitioner, ensure that he or she is registered and specializes in working with babies and children.

Questions & Answers

Whenever my baby cries more than usual, I always fret that he may be ill. My biggest fear is meningitis. How will I know?
This is a rare and extremely serious illness, but babies can recover with antibiotics if it is caught early. So if you ever suspect it, **take your baby to hospital immediately**. There are viral and bacterial types, and signs to look out for are a high-pitched, moaning cry, a very high temperature and your baby appearing sleepy or refusing to eat. One type, meningococcal meningitis, produces a red or purplish rash that doesn't fade when pressed with the side of a clear glass or your finger. Other types do not produce a rash, so never wait for this sign – seek medical help **as soon as possible**. There are vaccinations for meningitis C and *Haemophilus influenzae* type b (Hib).

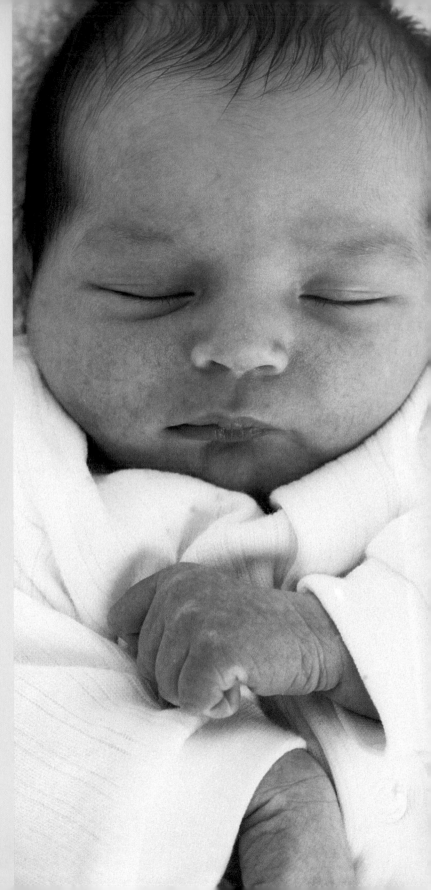

" I love to watch my baby when he's asleep. Sometimes he lies **still and peaceful**, and other times he **wriggles and twitches**. He even smiles as though he's having a lovely dream. **"**

EVA, mother of three-week-old Jake

The importance of sleep in the first months

Sleep is a precious commodity – both for your baby and for you. And it's not just the quantity of sleep that's important, it's the quality, too. Sleep affects every aspect of our lives, and understanding what happens when we sleep is the first step to helping your baby develop healthy sleeping habits that will benefit the whole family.

Sleep stages

Your baby's days are divided into periods of sleep and wakefulness. His sleep periods consist of two distinct states, which are very similar to those stages that we all experience.

• **Active sleep (so-called in newborn babies), also known as rapid–eye–movement (REM) sleep** Although the full function of REM sleep remains a mystery, it is known to be essential to the development and maintenance of the brain.

Newborn babies spend around half their sleep time in REM sleep, whereas in adulthood REM sleep accounts only for approximately 25 per cent of our sleep.

• **Quiet sleep (newborns) or non-REM sleep** Your baby's sleep is more peaceful and his brain is less active. Non-REM sleep consists of four phases of gradually deepening sleep: drowsiness, light sleep, deep sleep and very deep sleep. Your baby will go through these phases in "cycles", alternating periods of REM and non-REM sleep. During the progression into deepest sleep, your baby is less active and his breathing slows. Unlike during REM sleep, very little, if any, dreaming occurs in this stage.

Sleep cycles

Your newborn sleeps in cycles of around 50 or 60 minutes of REM and non-REM sleep. These cycles become longer as he matures. Like you, your baby wakes up several times in the

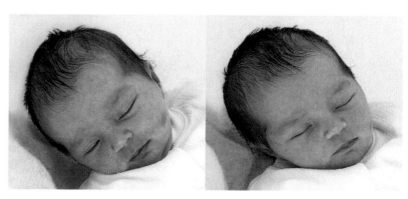

REM AND NON-REM SLEEP
Your newborn spends around half the time that he's asleep in REM sleep (left). During this stage, his eyes flick beneath his eyelids, or he may twitch his fingers and toes. The rest of the time, he's in deep, non-REM sleep (right), when he's very quiet and still.

Questions & Answers

Do premature babies have different sleep patterns?

Yes. Premature babies tend to wake more often at night than full-term infants for the first few months, and possibly up to a year. Night waking and lighter sleep are part of a premature baby's in-built survival mechanism in that he's able to wake easily so that he can be fed. He will sleep much more than a full-term baby, and a larger proportion of his sleep time (up to 90 per cent) will be spent in REM sleep. His sleep patterns will settle in time, but they will take longer than those of a baby born at term.

Does my baby dream?

It is not known for sure whether babies dream, but it seems very likely. Dreams take place during REM sleep, and babies spend a large part of their sleep time in this sleep stage. Experts are not entirely sure why we dream; some believe that it helps the brain to process information and exercise the synapses, or pathways, between brain cells. Interestingly, our brain waves during dream sleep, as recorded by machines, are almost identical in nature to the brain waves during the hours we spend awake. This is not the case during the other phases of sleep.

night as part of his natural sleep cycle. If he is able to lull himself back to sleep, this stirring will pass unnoticed. If he can't go back to sleep without help from you, he may become fully awake and cry. This is a common reason for disturbed nights and one that can be solved by teaching your baby how to soothe himself back to sleep.

How many hours?

Parents commonly ask how much sleep their baby needs. The answer is not straightforward, because every baby's sleep needs are different. Newborns have no regular pattern

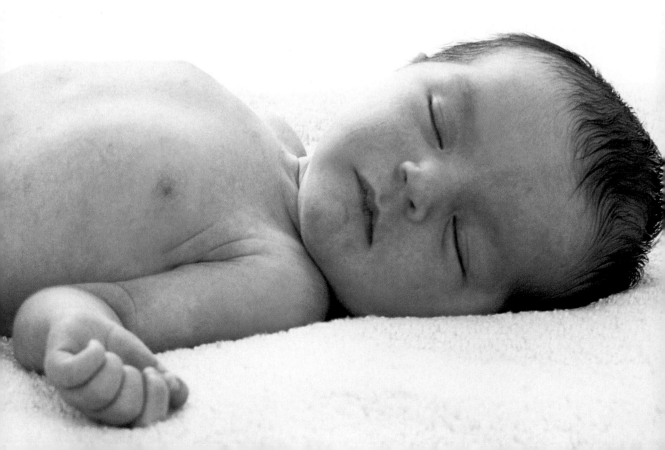

and may sleep from as little as 10½ hours to 20 hours out of 24. From two to three months, night-time sleep averages about nine hours, with around an additional five hours of naps through the day. By 12 months, your baby's night-time sleep will be around 11½ hours, with around 2½ hours of naps.

Evolving patterns

By around eight to 12 weeks, you may notice your baby's sleep becoming more regular, and you will be able to start guiding him into a day-night sleep routine. He may naturally begin to show a preference for night-time sleeping at this stage, and he'll probably spend longer periods awake and active during the day.

Healthy habits

Although your baby doesn't need to be taught how to sleep, healthy sleep habits are something he will have to learn. Whether he sleeps soundly or not depends to a great extent on what you teach him. This is not as daunting as it may sound, and the sooner you start, the easier it will be.

● **Establish a routine** Babies, toddlers and children are comforted by familiarity (see page 72). Regular bedtime habits – bathing, followed by feeding, cuddling and a little quiet time in the cot, for example – will

help your baby understand that soon it will be time to go to sleep.

● **Teach your baby to fall asleep by himself** This is one of the most valuable lessons you can teach your baby. Many experts believe that, after the newborn phase, putting your baby to bed by rocking him or feeding him prevents him from developing self-soothing behaviours. Instead, they recommend putting your baby to bed when he's still awake, well-fed, sleepy and able to fall asleep without help from you.

● **Make sure he gets daytime rest** Although it is a good idea to limit the length of daytime naps to maintain a contrast between night and day, keeping your baby awake when he wants to sleep makes him

A RELAXING BATH
Many babies find a warm bath relaxing, which makes it a perfect way to end the day as part of a bedtime routine.

overtired. He will then be harder to settle, and he will sleep more fitfully.

● **Be aware of your baby's needs** Respond quickly to a sudden change in your baby's sleep pattern. If he is teething or has a cold, you may need to alter his bedtime and naptime routines. An ill baby needs plenty of extra care. Once he's well again, return to your established routine.

● **Be consistent** Changing your baby's daytime routines and allowing him to sleep in different places is fine once in a while, but if it happens too often it can become a habit and lead to problems.

Expert tips

Cot safety

● Make sure the cot you choose for your baby is safety approved. Modern cot designs are required by law to meet certain standards.

● Cot bars should be no more than 6cm (2³/8in) apart, to prevent your baby's head and limbs getting stuck.

● Most cots have an adjustable mattress level, starting at its highest for easy access in the first months and finishing on the lowest level once your baby is able to sit up. There must be at least 50cm (20in) between the top of the mattress and the top of the cot in the lowest position and 20cm (8in) in the highest position.

● There should not be horizontal bars, which may allow your baby to climb up and possibly fall out.

● Every time you put your baby in her cot, check that the drop-side mechanism is locked. Never leave your baby in her cot with the side down.

The mattress

● The cot mattress should fit tightly – if you can slide two fingers between the cot sides or ends and the mattress, the mattress is too small.

● Mattresses are made of foam or natural fibres. Either is fine, as long as the mattress is firm, and fits snugly.

● Keep your baby's mattress well aired and clean. Mattresses with a PVC surface or a removable washable cover are easiest to keep clean.

Where should she sleep?

New babies are better off sleeping near their parents during the early weeks. You might prefer to start by having your baby in a Moses basket beside your bed, and move her into her own room when she is more settled. Moses baskets are cosy and practical. A good Moses basket should be firm but snug for your baby. They usually come with a valance that makes a frill around the outside, a liner and a mattress. Check that the mattress is a close fit (see left). Once your baby begins to roll, or is too long for the basket, it's time to move her to a cot.

Cradles

You may choose to use a cradle in the early months instead of a Moses

A MOSES BASKET

A Moses basket is the ideal size for your new baby, and can be carried from room to room, if necessary – although never when your baby is inside it!

basket. Cradles have many of the advantages of Moses baskets, but they are not portable. The main difference is that they can be rocked, and your newborn may find this very soothing. If you choose a rocking cradle, make sure you can lock it into a stationary position while your baby is sleeping, and that it cannot be tipped over.

Choosing a cot

Your baby can sleep in a cot from the start, but you may prefer to wait until she is past the newborn stage before you transfer her from her Moses basket or cradle. You can expect your baby to sleep in a cot until she's at least 18 months old, and maybe up to three years. You will know when she has outgrown it because she'll start trying to climb out of it!

There are several points to consider when choosing a cot.

● **Sturdiness** Once your baby is able to sit up and move around, a sturdy cot is a must.

● **Drop sides** One or both of the cot sides should drop for easy access. The catch mechanism needs to be very sturdy, because you will soon have a baby who can jump up and down and rattle the bars.

DROP SIDES
The drop-side mechanism on your baby's cot should be easy to operate, preferably with one hand, yet secure. Never leave the side down when your baby is in the cot.

● **Teething rails** Once she can stand, your baby may want to try out her new teeth on the top of her cot. Most cots have rigid plastic strips along the top rails to protect her from splinters. These strips also prevent the cot from being damaged.

● **Castors** Some cots are sold with castors, which make them easier to move around for cleaning. Ensure that the castors can be locked.

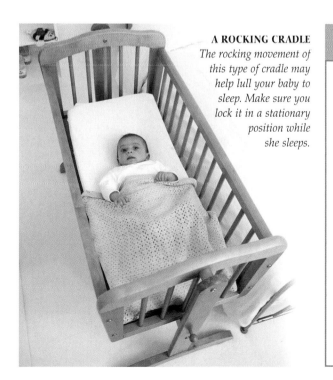

A ROCKING CRADLE
The rocking movement of this type of cradle may help lull your baby to sleep. Make sure you lock it in a stationary position while she sleeps.

Multi-purpose designs

Instead of a conventional cot, you may decide to choose a cot that is designed to meet specific needs.

● **A bedside cot** has a removable side so that it can become an extension of your bed at night. This is becoming an increasingly popular way of co-sleeping with a baby.

● **A rocking cradle** can be rocked, which many babies will find soothing, or it can be locked into static mode.

● **A cot-bed** can be used as a large cot in the early years and then, by removing the sides, can be transformed into a small bed when your child is old enough. It is a good idea, but a cot-bed is usually more expensive than a normal cot, and you will at some stage need to buy a full-size bed for your child. Also, as your family grows, you might need the cot again for another baby while your older child is still using it as a bed.

How can I keep my baby safe?

All parents worry about the possibility of Sudden Infant Death Syndrome (SIDS), but it's important to remember that the chances of it happening to your baby are very slim. The causes of this tragic syndrome are not yet fully understood, but there are some important precautions you can take to reduce the risk significantly.

The following recommendations apply throughout your baby's first year, although they are particularly important during the first six months, when incidences of SIDS are at their highest. If your baby sleeps with a babysitter or any other carer, make sure they also follow these guidelines.

FEET TO FOOT
Always place your baby with her feet to the foot of the cot, cradle or Moses basket. This safety measure ensures that she cannot slip under or become entangled with her bedclothes, if you are using them, and allows her to wriggle free of her covers if she becomes too hot.

★ **Always put your baby down to sleep on her back** Studies have proved that putting your baby to sleep on her back significantly lowers the risk of SIDS. Once your baby is older, she will be able to turn herself onto her stomach. However, you should continue to put her to sleep on her back even if she does change position in the night.

★ **Never smoke around your baby** You should also keep her away from smoky atmospheres. Babies who are exposed to cigarette smoke are at a higher risk of dying from SIDS.

★ **Keep your baby's bedroom at the right temperature** A room temperature of around 18°C (65°F) is ideal. Over-heating can be life-threatening because your baby cannot yet regulate her own temperature properly. The best way to test if she is becoming too hot is to feel her bare tummy or the nape of her neck.

★ **Place her with her feet at the foot of the cot, Moses basket or cradle** This is vital, because it prevents your baby slipping under the covers and suffocating. You should always keep her head uncovered.

★ **Never use duvets, quilts or thick blankets**
Soft bedding can cause your baby to become over-
heated. It is best to use a sheet or one or two
layers of thin blankets that are securely tucked into
the sides and foot of the mattress, no higher than
your baby's chest. In warmer weather, take off a
layer or remove bedcovers altogether.

★ **Never use cot bumpers or a pillow** These
can contribute to over-heating, and can also
suffocate your baby. For similar reasons, you should
never leave soft toys in her cot or put your baby
to sleep on top of a cushion, bean bag or water-bed.
Also, avoid falling asleep with your baby on a sofa.

★ **Never use hot-water bottles** You should also
never use electric blankets in your baby's bed.

★ **Use a firm mattress, and clean and air
it regularly** Also make sure that there is no
gap between the edges and the sides of the cot
(see page 54).

★ **Seek medical advice promptly** if your
baby is unwell.

YOUR BABY'S BEDDING
*If you use bedding, use a sheet or one or two thin
blankets that reach no higher than your baby's
chest, securely tucked in on all sides.*

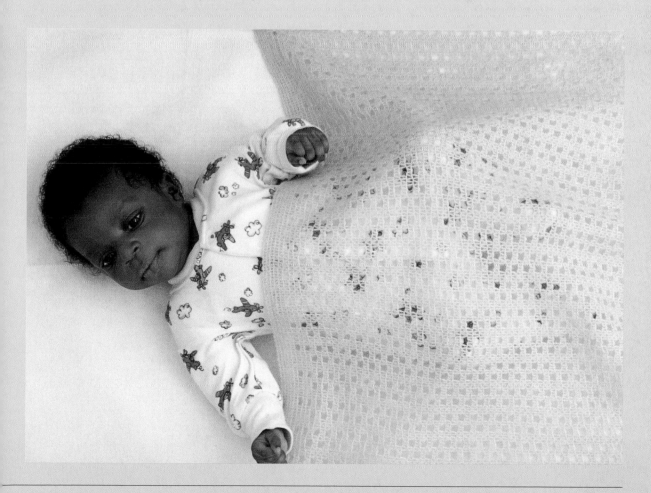

"Nathan feeds greedily to begin with, followed by little bursts of comfort sucks, before falling happily asleep."

MARTHA is mum to five-week-old Nathan

Your baby's movements

While sleeping, your baby may:

- be very busy twitching, jerking, sucking, snuffling or smiling. This is normal. Even with all this activity, he is getting a sound sleep. These movements happen when your baby is in REM, or "dream", sleep (see page 51)

- suddenly "jump" in his sleep occasionally. This is due to a normal reflex called the "startle" or Moro reflex. It sometimes occurs for no apparent reason, although often it is a response to a loud noise or sudden jolt. It may seem worrying to you, but the reflex is actually a reassuring sign that your baby's neurological system is functioning well. It will disappear by around four months.

The first few weeks

Wakefulness for the first few hours after birth, followed by a long stretch, often up to 24 hours, of very sound sleep, is the normal newborn pattern. At this stage, he will probably be alert only for short periods every day; he's not mature enough to benefit from longer periods of alertness, and sleep (particularly REM sleep) helps him to mature. Gradually, these periods of wakefulness will grow longer, so that by the end of the first month he may be awake for a total of around two or three hours every day, most of it in one long stretch. He may also begin to sleep for longer periods, so that, instead of one or two hours, he may be able to sleep for three or four.

Sleeping and feeding

It's natural for a newborn to fall asleep while sucking at the breast or on a bottle. After the first few weeks you may want to start to change this habit so that you put him down while he's still awake but drowsy. An experienced feeder will take most of his feed during the first five minutes or so, and once full may doze off at the breast or bottle in contentment. But if he hasn't emptied your breast or the bottle, gently wake him up after a few minutes and offer him some more. If he's still hungry, he'll finish his feed.

Paediatricians recommend that newborn babies should not sleep longer than three or four hours without feeding. At this stage, your baby needs a constant supply of nourishment and needs waking. If he doesn't wake up when you pick him up, try sitting him on your lap and gently bending him forwards. When he stirs, put him in a position ready to feed, with your nipple or the teat close to his lips. Try changing his nappy, tickling his feet, or brushing his cheek with your nipple or the teat. If all attempts fail, leave him a bit longer and then try again. But never let him go more than five hours without a feed.

Sleeping and crying

Your baby cries because it is the only way he can communicate – it's his way of telling you he's hungry, in pain, in need of a cuddle, or simply sleepy. At first, it's hard to interpret your baby's different cries, but as you get to know him, you'll respond to them more easily.

Using a dummy

So that the dummy does not become a habit, you should aim to use it only during the early months, and restrict it to bedtimes only. A dummy can soothe your baby to sleep, and comfort him. If he keeps hold of the dummy, he may be less likely to wake up after a disturbance or during the lighter stages of his sleep. However, dummies often fall out during sleep, disturbing your baby. He will probably start crying until you come and find it again. They can also limit sound-making, and may stop him exploring toys with his mouth later.

Inconsolable and excessive crying

A baby who cries regularly and inconsolably for long periods, usually at the end of the day, is often described as having "colic", which experts now believe may be simply an extreme form of normal crying. Your baby could be overtired or over-stimulated, and once he's started crying, he doesn't know how to stop.

It can be upsetting to see your baby in distress and not be able to soothe him, but colic is not serious, and it does no long-term damage. By three or four months, it will have stopped. A colicky baby may cry himself to sleep, but stay with him, preferably in a darkened, quiet room. Also:

- try a "colic dance", rocking him up and down while swaying your hips

- gently rub his abdomen, or pat his back while holding him across your forearm or up against your shoulder

- give him a bath, but stop if he becomes more agitated

- give him a relaxing massage.

A SOOTHING HOLD
Lay your baby across your forearm and, keeping a steadying grasp between his legs, gently rub or pat his back.

How can I help my newborn sleep?

Sometimes, your new baby will fall asleep at the drop of a hat, but there will be other occasions when he refuses to settle, waking up and crying every time you put him down. Bear in mind that he hasn't long left the warm, cosy and secure environment of your womb; it can take some time to adapt to his strange new world. The key to coping in the early days is to help him feel comfortable and secure, creating a soothing environment for him.

USE A SLING
The more you can hold your new baby close, the more secure and settled he'll be. A sling helps you carry him, while keeping both hands free.

Ways to soothe your newborn

★ **Calming movement** When he was in the womb, your baby was lulled by the motion of you going about your daily business. Out of the womb, movement still has this effect on him. Rocking, swaying and patting while cuddled up in your arms will all contribute to contentment – and sleep – during these early weeks. After a few months, it is best to help your baby to learn to self-soothe and fall asleep on his own. But for now, he needs you.

★ **Gentle sound** In the womb, your baby was used to hearing the comforting sounds of your heartbeat, the gurgling of your stomach, and the soft tones of your voice. Now he's born, sleeping may be difficult without some background noise. He might like you talking quietly, singing or humming to him. Or he may be soothed by the rhythmic hum of a fan or the washing machine or strains of music from a radio. You could even play him a recording of womb sounds.

★ **Helping him feel secure** Because your baby is used to being curled up in a tight space, the vast expanse of a cot may make him feel insecure. If your baby seems uncomfortable in a cot, then a cradle, a Moses basket or a pram can be used to provide a snug fit that's closer to the nine-month-long embrace in the womb. For added security, try swaddling (see page 37).

★ **A full tummy** If possible, try to make the last feed you give your baby before bedtime a full one. If he nods off before he has had enough, change his position, tickle his toes and rouse him so that he can finish the feed. Otherwise, you may find he will soon wake up again for his second course.

★ **Soothing smells** Your baby has a very keen sense of smell and, in particular, he will find your individual scent very comforting. So, you could try stuffing a muslin square or a handkerchief into your shirt for a short while so that it smells of you and then placing it safely in his cot, Moses basket or cradle.

SING TO HIM
He loves the sound of your voice, and he's trying hard to focus on your face. Try singing to him, and gently swaying your hips from side to side as you cradle him in your arms.

GO FOR A WALK
The fresh air and the sights and sounds of the great outdoors will soon tire your baby. He'll also be soothed by the steady movement of the pushchair.

A GOOD FEED
Your baby will settle well if he's feeling full. If he empties one breast and still seems hungry, offer him the other side. Try winding him before putting him down.

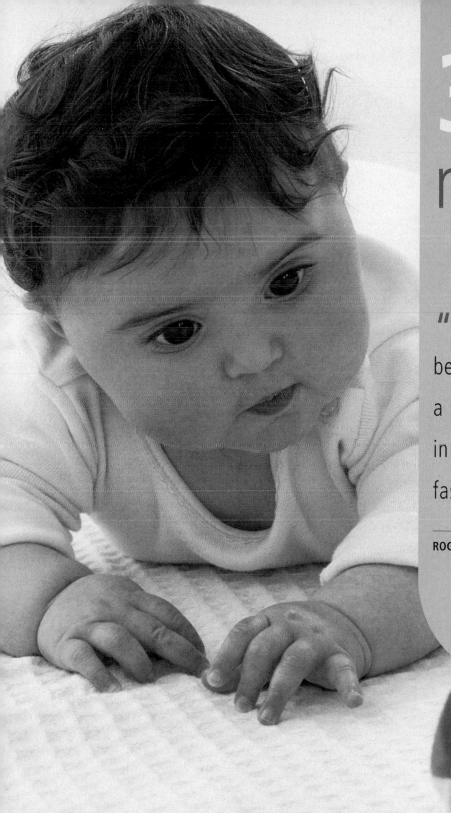

3-6
months

" She's now beginning to take **a real interest** in her toys, which is fascinating to watch. "

ROGER, father of four-month-old Keira

" Expressing my breast milk means that I have a little more **freedom** and time **for myself** while Tim feeds Matthew. "

JULIA, mother of four-month-old Matthew

Expressing breast milk

By the third month you will probably be feeling more confident about breastfeeding your baby: feeding should be settling into a pattern, and any early problems that you may have encountered will hopefully have been resolved. You may also be thinking about expressing milk for your baby at around this time.

What does expressing mean?

In a perfect world no mother would ever have to be apart from her baby – but sometimes babies and their mothers can't be together. When this is the case, direct mother-to-child feeding isn't the only option: if you are separated from your baby, expressing milk provides an alternative means of giving her breast milk.

Expressing means squeezing the milk out of your breasts. It's done either by hand, or using an electric or manual pump. The milk is then stored in bottles or bags in the fridge or freezer to be used whenever your baby needs feeding and you aren't around to do it directly.

When babies and their mothers can't be together it is usually for one of two reasons. In some instances a baby may need to be cared for intensively in a special care baby unit. This may be because she was born prematurely, because she didn't grow properly in the uterus or because she has some other medical problem that needs to be treated.

A second reason for expressing might be if the mother chooses or feels she has no choice but to go back to work outside the home, and is unable to have her baby looked after on or close to her employer's premises. In either of these cases, being able to express milk which is then fed to the baby when the mother isn't around makes the difference between having to stop breastfeeding and being able to carry on.

There is a third category of mothers who might want to learn to express: those who have occasional reason to be apart from their babies – this might be a day away, or perhaps an overnight trip when they can leave their babies with others.

Expressing if your baby is in special care

This is the hardest situation in which to express because, unlike a mother who's returning to work and who's already an experienced breastfeeder, you'll be starting your life as a breastfeeding mother with only a pump to get the milk to flow. Emotionally you'll be in a difficult situation – your pregnancy has probably ended in an entirely unexpected way, and now you find

Expert tip

Hand expression (see page 66) is a useful skill for any breastfeeding mother to master. For example, you can relieve the pressure of engorged breasts by expressing some milk gently while sitting in a warm bath. And rubbing a little expressed milk onto a sore or cracked nipple can help it to heal.

How do I express?

Expression techniques depend on whether you're using a pump or expressing by hand. Remember that practice is hugely important – this is an entirely learned skill, and the more you do it the more efficient and confident you will become. Some people find having a warm shower or bath before they start can encourage the milk to flow.

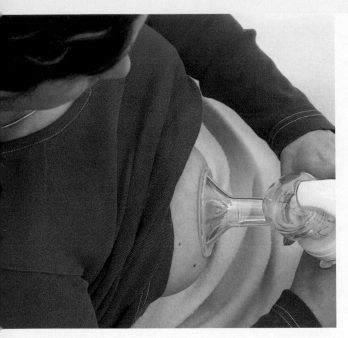

will start to drip from your breasts. At the first few pumping sessions you're unlikely to come away with more than a few drops. But over time your efforts will result in a lot more milk being collected.

Hand expression

Hand expression is a useful skill. Wash your hands before you start. Then place your thumbs above your nipple and your fingers below so they form a circle around your areola. Squeeze gently, pushing the glands behind the areola in a circular motion. Use a sterile bowl to collect the milk. Hand expressing is time-consuming at first, but some women go on to be experts and find it almost as efficient as a pump.

Pump expression

Whether you're using an electric, battery-operated or manual pump, you'll start by holding the cup and bottle attachment to your nipple, ensuring as much of the areola as possible is covered with the cup.

Switch the machine on or, if you are using a hand pump, start to activate the suction process with the handle. The suction mimics the way a baby sucks at the nipple, drawing it out rhythmically, and milk

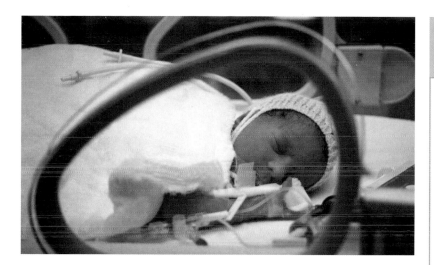

SPECIAL-CARE BABIES
If your baby was in special care, you may have had to express your breast milk so that she got the best possible nourishment at such a crucial time.

yourself with a tiny baby who might be in hospital for a long time, and who you'd desperately like to go on to breastfeed.

Premature babies either can't suck or can't suck very efficiently – they are just too little to do so, because they have been born before the sucking reflex has been properly developed. The milk you express can only be fed into your baby's tiny body by tube – you'll probably be able to assist in this by holding the tube during the feed. Because your breasts are being stimulated only via the pump, you need to express regularly and often. Keeping your supply going will be one of the biggest challenges. To assist this you could try the following:

● getting a special "dual cup" attachment for your breast pump, so that you can express milk from both breasts at the same time – this helps increase your milk production by making your body think you're feeding two babies

● waking at night to express – this increases your supply because your levels of prolactin, which switches on the milk-producing cells in your breasts, are higher at night

● looking at a picture of your baby while you are expressing – this will actually encourage your milk to let down

● going back to the first breast a second time after you've expressed from the second side, when you're using a single cup attachment.

Which kind of breast pump?

● **Hospital-grade electric pumps**
Best for mothers whose babies are in hospital. These pumps, which are expensive and therefore usually available to hire, are the best substitute for a baby's suck in efficiently removing milk from the breast. If your baby is in a special care unit and is too small or too weak to suck at all directly from you, this sort of pump will keep your milk supply up until your baby is old enough and strong enough to learn to do it herself.

● **Mains-operated portable pumps**
These provide a means for expressing at home for a mother who's spending much of her time in hospital with her baby. They're also useful for working mothers who need to express often.

● **Battery-operated pumps**
These are not as strong as either of the above pumps, but they are light and easy to carry and a useful back-up for a working mother who needs to travel away from her office sometimes.

● **Hand-operated pumps**
These work by squeezing a handle to produce a vacuum in a cup attached to your nipple, encouraging the milk to flow. They are more time-consuming than other pumps, and also harder work, but are useful for mothers who want to express only occasionally or who want to try it without a big financial outlay.

How can I store my milk?

You'll need to put your expressed milk in special plastic bottles or in plastic bags made for the purpose. Remember to write the date on the bag. You need to ensure your milk is stored in sterilized containers: you can boil them for 10 minutes, or use sterilizing tablets; alternatively, buy a steam sterilizer. If you are using bottles to feed your baby expressed milk, these will have to be carefully cleaned using special brushes and sterilized – milk harbours germs, so don't overlook this.

Fresh milk stored in the fridge should be used within 24 hours. Frozen milk lasts up to three months, and up to 24 hours once defrosted. Freezing does destroy some of the antibodies in milk, so use fresh expressed milk whenever possible. But even thawed milk is a lot better than formula in terms of its health-giving properties.

MILK STORAGE
You can store your milk in special plastic bags or bottles.

Put the bottle or bag of frozen milk into a bowl of warm water to thaw, or defrost in the fridge overnight. Don't use a microwave for expressed milk as it will kill some of the nutrients. And even though you might be tempted not to, always throw away any remaining expressed milk at the end of a feed – don't keep it for a later feed as it may harbour germs.

Expressing if you are going back to work

Expressing is a good option if you're returning to work while your baby is still relatively young – maybe as little as three or four months – and is still exclusively breastfed. If you can delay your return to work until after six months when she'll be taking some solid food in addition to breast milk, you may be able to adjust your feeding schedule so you increase the number of feeds she has when you're together, and gets by with formula from a cup or bottle when you're at work.

Planning expression

Expressing is time-consuming and can be a complicated procedure to set up for a workplace, but it does ensure that your baby can have as

Questions & Answers

I'm going back to work in eight weeks. Should I start to express?
Start getting used to expressing and build up a good freezer supply of milk a few weeks before you go back to work. Knowing you are adept at expressing will make you a lot more confident about your return. Also, knowing there are plenty of bottles of milk in the freezer will take the pressure off you to produce lots of milk once you are back at work.

My baby is in a special care unit and will be for at least a month. How often should I express?
The answer to this depends on your individual ability to produce milk – some women need more breast stimulation than others to do this successfully. As a rough guide, you will probably need to express between six and eight times in 24 hours. Do consider expressing at night if your milk production seems to be going down, as this will give it a boost.

How long should each session expressing with an electric breast pump take?
As time goes on you will become increasingly efficient at expressing, but you probably need to spend at least 30 minutes at a time with the pump. It's worth stopping and starting, and switching sides, for maximum effect. When you first start using a pump the trick is to go for frequent, short sessions.

much breast milk as she needs, even when you're not physically with her.

Becoming a working mother who expresses takes some organizing. Start while you're still pregnant by preparing the ground at your workplace for the expressing sessions you'll need to start once you go back.

Talk to your supervisor, and explain that while you're committed to a return to work, you're also committed to breastfeeding. Tell the supervisor that many other women have managed to achieve what you're hoping for, and reassure her that it won't affect your ability to do your job. In fact, many women who express while at work say they find it easier to concentrate on their work because they know that although they can't be with their child, they're doing their very best for her.

How will it work?

It's best to think through very carefully where you will express at work, and where you will store your milk, before you talk to your supervisor. Unless you're in the fortunate position where other women in your workplace regularly express, it may be a new issue for your superiors and it's best if you go prepared with the answers to the many queries they are likely to have.

STAY-AT-HOME DADS
If your partner is caring for your baby because you have gone back to work, expressed milk ensures your baby can continue to have the best possible nutrition from her other parent.

These will probably include:
● Where will you express your breast milk? You will need a reasonably comfortable space where you can be assured privacy.
● Where will you store the milk? You'll need a fridge – you might want to consider investing in your own mini-fridge to keep your milk out of view from your colleagues.
● Will your breast pump remain on your work premises, and if so will it be insured?
● How much time do you anticipate expressing is going to take out of your working day?

" We've hung a brightly coloured **musical mobile** over Susannah's cot. I always turn it on as I say goodnight, and she usually falls asleep listening to its gentle **lullaby**."

JAN, mother of four-month-old Susannah

Encouraging good sleep habits

At around two to three months old, you may see a change in your baby's sleeping patterns. She will probably have more periods during the day when she's showing an interest in her surroundings. At night, she may be sleeping for longer stretches. This is the ideal time to start to encourage her to adopt good sleeping habits.

Changing patterns

By now, your baby will be alert for longer periods during the day, and she may also be starting to sleep for longer stretches at night. A rhythm to her sleeping and waking times will soon emerge and, over the coming weeks, you will probably see these patterns taking a definite shape.

At six months old, most babies' sleep is consolidated into one longer sleep at night and several shorter sleeps during the day. There are a number of factors that contribute to these changes in your baby's sleeping patterns.

• Her sleep-wake cycles are becoming less dependent on hunger: as her stomach capacity grows, she can go longer without needing to feed. She may even drop one of her night feeds altogether. By six months,

when solid foods account for a substantial part of their diet, most – but not all – babies will sleep for a six-hour stretch without waking.

• Your baby's internal body clock is beginning to tick. This means that she will spend more time awake during the day and more time asleep at night. Her body clock is regulated by internal factors like hunger and tiredness, as well as external ones, such as light and dark, and her day-to-day routine.

• Her mental and social skills are developing so that she is able to recognize and respond to your cues. For example, if you give her a bath before bedtime every night, she will now have the capacity to remember that after a bath, it's time for her to settle down and go to sleep.

Expert tips

Between two and six months, your baby will give you cues that she is getting sleepy and is ready for a nap or bedtime. She may:

• decrease her level of activity and go quiet

• lose interest in people or toys

• start yawning

• rub her eyes

• look "glazed"

• become fussy or irritable

• bury her head in your chest or turn away from you.

Checklist

Your baby's bedtime routine can include any (or all) of the following activities:

- giving her a bath
- giving her a gentle massage
- putting on her sleepsuit
- reading a bedtime story
- singing to her
- cuddling her
- feeding her
- kissing her goodnight.

Helping your baby sleep

From around three months, you can help teach your baby to adopt healthy sleep patterns by doing two very important things:

- gently teaching her how to go to sleep by herself, and
- establishing a bedtime routine.

At some point, you will want your baby to feel secure enough to go to sleep and stay asleep without needing you there (see below). If she is able to do this, she will sleep better, which will have a positive impact on her physical and mental development. It also means that you and your whole family will reap the rewards – eventually – by having fewer disturbed nights.

Starting a routine

When your baby was a newborn, deciding when to put her down for the night was as easy as watching for the signs of sleepiness she gave, such as crying, yawning or rubbing her eyes.

While your baby may still do these things (and you should still respond to them), you don't need to wait for

Steps to a good night's sleep

1 For your baby to learn how to sleep by herself, she needs to be put to bed while she is still awake. Instead of rocking her to sleep or allowing her to doze off while feeding, keep her awake: sing or talk to her in a soft voice, stroke her head, or cuddle her.

2 When she is drowsy, put her into her cot on her back. At first, she may become more awake and fuss or cry. Soothe her gently, say goodnight in a soft voice and leave.

3 If she cries, resist going back for a few minutes. If she carries on, go in to her, stroke her, but don't pick her up.

4 When she is calm, leave the room again. If she continues to cry, wait a little longer than last time, then repeat the soothing visit. You may have to do this many times, but if you are consistent, within a few nights she will be going to sleep by herself. Some babies go to sleep with the help of a soothing sensation, such as sucking a thumb or dummy (see page 59). Others prefer the feel of a soft toy or blanket. Never put your baby to bed with a bottle, as this can cause tooth decay.

5 If your baby wakes during the night, and she is not due a feed or crying out of pain or discomfort, repeat these steps, waiting for a few minutes before soothing her and leaving the room again.

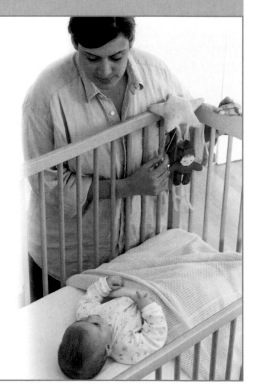

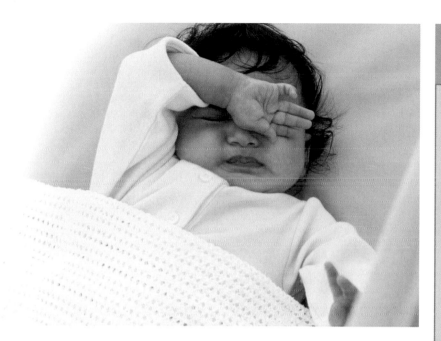

these signs before you put her to bed. You can now take more control of bedtimes, by putting her down at roughly the same time every night, with a similar routine.

To begin with, this will be a bit hit and miss because her feeding and napping habits can still be unpredictable. But introducing a routine now can go a long way towards regulating these patterns and setting her body clock to a healthy schedule.

She will probably respond well to routine at this stage, and enjoy the rituals of preparing for her night-time sleep.

The following tips will help you establish a bedtime routine that works for both you and your baby.

● **Choose your baby's bedtime** – and try to stick to it whenever possible. Normally, this will be any time between 7pm and 8.30pm. If you put her to bed any later than 8.30pm, there is a risk that she may become overtired.

● **Be consistent** Try to follow the same sequence of events at around the same time every evening.

● **Always keep your routine manageable** Elaborate routines can become drawn out indefinitely, which means that you will be spending longer than necessary settling your baby to sleep and defeats the object of the exercise.

● **Try to stick to a daytime routine, too** Your baby will now have longer periods of wakefulness

Questions & Answers

Should I let my baby fall asleep at the breast?
It's natural for a baby to fall asleep while sucking at the breast or on a bottle. While it's fine to let your newborn do this, if it becomes a habit, over time she will learn to associate sucking with falling asleep, and may eventually not be able to fall asleep in any other way. If you want your baby to be able to go to sleep without your help, remove the breast or bottle when she appears to be dropping off. At first, your baby may resist and start to fuss and try to find the nipple or teat again. Let her do this, but as she starts to fall asleep again, remove the nipple or teat again. You may need to repeat this many times, but eventually, your baby will learn how to fall asleep without a nipple or teat in her mouth.

during the day, so you will have the opportunity to give the day more of a structure. Having regular times for playing, feeding and napping, for example, can be beneficial for you and your baby.

● **Be flexible** Having a routine doesn't mean you have to stick to it rigidly. It will vary sometimes, depending on what you're doing in the day and how tired your baby is. Be consistent, but know when to bend the rules.

How can I help my baby settle at night – and sleep through?

A bedtime routine helps your baby recognize that it's time to go to sleep – and the ideal time to start a simple routine is from around the age of three months. Once she is settled, there are steps you can take to ensure that she doesn't wake up unnecessarily.

Starting a routine

Think carefully about what you would like to include in your young baby's bedtime routine, because whatever you establish now may later become a habit that will be hard to break. You can always add to her routine as she gets older (see pages 116–117) but, for now, keep it simple. Your aim should be to create a peaceful, relaxing end to her increasingly busy day. Try the following:

★ **A warm bath** As well as a practical way of keeping her clean, a gentle splash in the water before bed can be enjoyable.

★ **A massage** Massage is known to boost a baby's feeling of wellbeing, and is a perfect way to help her relax before bed, especially after her bath.

★ **A cuddle and a feed** Once she's dressed, a cuddle and a good feed will help her go to bed contentedly. Try to ensure that you put her down awake, but drowsy.

A BATH
A bath can help your baby to wind down. Make sure the bathroom is warm and have a towel, a fresh nappy and her sleepsuit to hand. Wrap her up and give her a big hug!

Why is she waking?

Erratic sleep patterns are normal during the early months, but you can start to help your baby sleep through the night by considering why she's waking and trying to eliminate the cause.

★ **Is she hungry?** If she suddenly starts waking more frequently she may be having a growth spurt, which means she needs more milk to be sustained.

★ **Is she uncomfortable?** Always check that your baby is not in pain, that her nappy is not wet or soiled, or that she's not too hot or cold (see pages 56–57). Check for a temperature, and other signs of illness. If you suspect she is ill, call your doctor.

★ **Is she being disturbed?** If she sleeps in your room, she may hear you stirring, for example, so think about moving her to her own room.

★ **Is her room too dark or too light?**
Your baby needs just enough light to reassure herself that she's in familiar surroundings. A simple night-light can solve this problem. Black-out curtains will help block out light.

★ **Are you sure she's really awake?**
Sometimes, you may think your baby is waking when she's just in a phase of light sleep. Or she may be awake but about to drift back to sleep if not stimulated. When you know she's not ill or hungry, let her fuss for a few minutes before going to her.

★ **Can she fall asleep by herself?**
Putting her down while drowsy but still awake will help her learn to fall asleep by herself (see page 72).

A MASSAGE
Massage your baby using light, circular or sweeping strokes all over her body, and a little baby oil if you wish. As you massage her, talk softly to her and maintain eye contact.

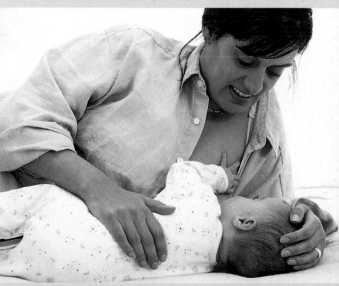

A CUDDLE AND A FEED
Make sure that the last feed your baby has before bedtime is a full feed, so that she doesn't wake up too soon feeling hungry. If she falls asleep before she has finished, try to rouse her.

Coping with early risers

If your baby regularly wakes up too early in the morning, you can sometimes solve the problem by putting black-out curtains or blinds on the window in her room to block out the morning light. Don't go to her straight away when she wakes up and fusses – leave her a while to see if she will go back to sleep.

Some paediatricians recommend helping your baby "readjust" her body clock, by keeping her up an extra hour at night, but there is no guarantee that this will work.

If you do try it, it's worth persisting for several nights to see if there is a difference to her waking time because any change won't take effect immediately.

Unfortunately, many babies and children are simply unable to sleep late in the morning and wake just because they have had enough sleep. You may have to adapt to her pattern for a while. At around six months, you can put some of her favourite toys in her cot to keep her occupied while you catch a few more precious minutes of sleep.

Daytime naps

The length and quality of your baby's daytime naps will affect her night-time sleep – and vice versa. By four or five months, the typical baby takes three or four regular naps of an hour or so each during the day. Some babies will take two longer ones of around 90 minutes or more.

Longer naps may be more beneficial for your baby; cat-napping during the day – falling asleep in sporadic bursts of half an hour or so – does not have the same effect, and your baby may follow the same pattern during the night, waking up frequently. So, try to encourage your baby to sleep better during the day.

● Aim to time her naps well. Having a nap too late in the day can mean that she won't sleep as well at night.

Questions & Answers

How do I know whether my baby is getting enough sleep?
Many babies regulate themselves pretty well when it comes to getting their quota of sleep, but not every baby gets as much as she needs. If she is frequently irritable and hard to please, it may be that your baby isn't napping enough or getting enough total sleep. If you believe your baby needs more sleep, try putting her down earlier, even if she cries for a while, and leaving her for a few minutes if she wakes in the night or too early in the morning to see if she goes back to sleep. But if she sleeps less than the "average" for her age and seems happy, then she's probably getting enough sleep and just happens not to need as much as other babies.

LONGER NAPS
It's better for your baby to have longer naps of good-quality sleep, than to snatch several short sleeps during the day.

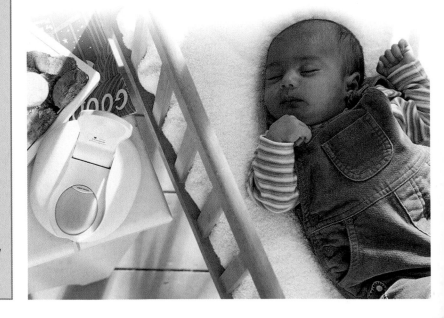

Incidentally, cutting down on daytime naps won't help her to sleep more at night – in fact, it can be a recipe for overtiredness and lead to your baby having a worse night's sleep.

- As soon as you know that your baby is tired, let her sleep. If she gets overtired, she may become irritable and find it very hard to sleep.
- Plan a nap routine to help her wind down. A feed or drink, a look at a book and a cuddle before putting her down will be enough.
- Make sure that she has a comfortable place to nap. Letting her fall asleep on your shoulder will be uncomfortable for you, and will mean that she doesn't sleep for long – her cot is better.
- Check that she isn't too warm or too cold (see pages 56–57).
- Try not to let her fall asleep just before her feed is due because she will probably wake up too soon out of hunger.
- Change her nappy before you put her down so that she feels comfortable as she settles.
- Play and interact with your baby when she's awake and active between naps. At five months, she should be able to stay awake for around three hours at a stretch – but with so much to hold her interest now, don't let her get overtired.

Snoring and noisy breathing

From around eight weeks, or sometimes before, some babies start to make "snoring" noises in their sleep. These are caused by loose mucus in the nose and throat (common in young babies) and may be accompanied by a rattling in her chest, which you may be able to feel with your hand. You may also notice a pause in your baby's breathing for a short period.

Some babies have more of a throat gurgle, usually the result of having a soft and flexible airway. This resolves itself within a year or two as the rings of cartilage in the airway become more rigid.

These snoring sounds do not usually interfere with your baby's breathing and will disappear over the next few weeks.

Always have any breathing irregularities, snores, gurgles or pauses in your baby's breathing checked by your doctor. Although it is unlikely to be a serious problem, other causes need to be ruled out. If your baby suddenly starts making strange breathing sounds or wheezes, see your doctor promptly.

" I love it now that Megan's more active during the day, but she gets tired easily. So, as soon as she starts rubbing her eyes, I put her down. "

SUE, mum to six-month-old Megan

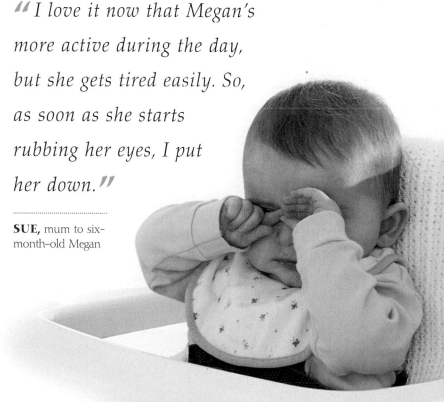

" I love breastfeeding Eve. I'm also **excited** about giving her some solid food. She already enjoys **sitting with us** at mealtimes. "

LIZ, mother of five-month-old Eve

Getting ready for solids

Breast milk is the perfect food for your baby for the first year. But, as she grows, milk alone is no longer enough. For healthy physical development your baby needs to learn how to eat solid food. This is also the first step towards feeding herself and joining in family meals.

Why does your baby need solid food?

As your baby gets bigger she needs more calories to maintain her rate of growth. If she stays on a diet of milk alone she'll have to feed more often and her needs will not be satisfied.

Solid food can give your baby the extra calories she needs without filling her up too quickly. It can also give her the extra nutrients her body now requires. For example, from six months your baby's natural supply of iron is starting to dwindle. Iron is vital for healthy growth and milk alone cannot provide her with enough.

Introducing your baby to solids is also her first step towards enjoying healthy food and discovering that sharing meals is fun. Your baby is becoming more independent – she is learning how to sit up unaided and to grab what she wants; she loves to put things in her mouth, and she wants to be included in everything.

Learning how to eat solid food and joining in family meals is the next step on her journey to independence.

When to start

The recommended ideal age to start getting your baby used to solids has traditionally been between four and six months. However, experts now believe that babies need nothing more than breast milk for the first six months of their lives. If your baby seems dissatisfied after her usual milk feed and is less than six months old, try to satisfy her by breastfeeding more often or talk to your health visitor. Whether you are breastfeeding or bottle-feeding formula, around six months weaning should commence.

In order for your baby to accept, swallow and digest solid food, certain physical developments need to occur:
● loss of the tongue-thrust reflex – at birth your baby naturally pushes anything that goes into her mouth

out again with her tongue, but between four and six months this reflex disappears
● development of her jaw and tongue so she can move food to the back of her mouth ready to swallow
● development of coordination and head control so she can maintain the posture needed for swallowing
● maturity of the gastrointestinal tract so she can digest different foods
● the ability to cope with a larger volume of food in her tummy.

Checklist

Your baby needs to start eating solid food because:

● milk alone can no longer satisfy her physical needs

● her stores of iron are running out so she needs an additional source

● eating solid food is fun – and your baby wants to be one of the family!

Is my baby ready for solids?

Your baby will be ready for solids some time around six months of age. There is no hard and fast rule – as with other skills, such as sitting up or crawling, some babies are ready to move on earlier than others. The deciding factor should be your own baby's needs and development. If you are unsure, talk to your health visitor or GP.

Don't start too soon

Until the age of six months, all your baby's nutritional needs are met by your breast milk. Between the ages of four and six months your baby loses her natural tongue-thrust reflex

NO NEED TO HURRY
If your baby has only been fed milk, by the time she is six months old she will be enthusiastic about trying something new.

(see page 79), and as her digestive system matures she will become able to cope with solid food – waiting until six months is especially important if you have a family history of allergies. Once she is approaching this age, start to watch out for the following signs.

★ **She seems more hungry than usual**
When your baby starts shortening the length of time between feeds or even starts waking in the night for an extra feed, chances are she could be ready to give solids a try.

★ **She can hold her head up well**
Your baby needs good head control before she can safely be given puréed foods, otherwise there is a risk of choking. By now she should be able to lift her head properly when she is propped up or strapped into a reclining chair.

★ **She's interested in the food you eat**
Watch your baby at the table. Is she following each bite you take? Does she look as if she's imitating you chewing? Does she make noises and wave her hands as if saying "Hey, can I have some?" By six months most babies are expressing a desire for solid food.

What about premature babies?

If your baby was born early, you need to be careful when calculating her age for starting solids. Avoid introducing them until at least four to six months after her due date rather than after her birthday.

Delaying the introduction of solids much beyond six months may cause problems later on, as teaching older infants to chew can be difficult. In addition, your baby may not be getting all the nutrients she needs from milk alone after this time. Consult your doctor or health visitor about when to start if you are unsure.

Once you feel your baby is ready to start solids, it's important to go at her pace. Your baby will – like all other babies – discover how to lift her head, swallow purée and eventually hold her own spoon and feed herself. But she is also unique and will do these things only when she is ready.

Your baby still needs milk

Your baby is not ready to give up the breast or bottle just because she starts eating solid food. To begin with she'll simply be getting used to new tastes and textures and much of what you put in her mouth will come straight back out, so she

"THAT LOOKS GOOD!"
When your baby starts showing interest in your food, you can be sure that she's getting ready to try some solids herself.

❝ Ben, my eldest, was a hungry baby. Within a couple of weeks of starting solids he was devouring everything in sight. Thomas was more laid back and took longer to get going – but now he loves mealtimes as much as his brother does. ❞

JAN is mum to Ben, 5, and Thomas, 3

still needs her full supply of breast milk or formula. In fact, this will be an important source of nutrition for her until she is one year old.

Experiencing solids

For your baby, tasting solids for the first time is an incredible experience. When you offer her her first tastes you are doing a lot more than just giving her the nourishment she needs – you are stimulating her senses in a way she has never experienced before.

HEAD CONTROL
Your baby's ability to hold his head up without support is a key sign that you will be able to start feeding him solid food before long.

● Taste

From an early age "tasting" is a way of exploring and as soon as your baby is able, everything within reach will be mouthed – although she may not always like the taste! She was born with a full set of 10,000 taste buds and, while they take some years to mature fully, she can already tell the difference between sweet and sour.

● Smell

Just as babies prefer sweet tastes, they also prefer sweet smells such

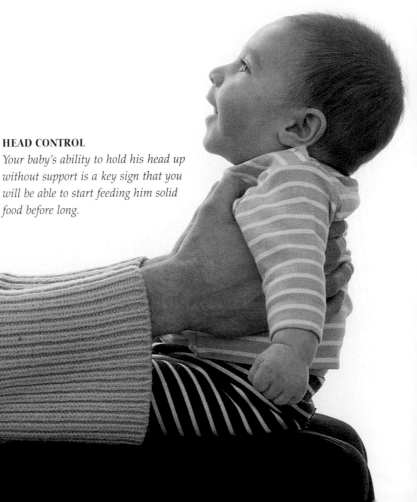

as vanilla and banana. In fact, your baby's sense of smell is so acute she is able to tell the difference between your breast milk and that of another mother. Smelling is another way in which your baby learns about the world around her – and giving her new foods offers her the chance to discover new smells.

● Touch

Feeling things with her mouth is one of the most important ways your baby has of exploring and learning about her environment. And food teaches her a lot about texture – it can be soft (mashed banana) or hard (a cube of cheese), rough (a rice biscuit) or smooth (a grape). Even a runny purée feels strangely different to your baby's mouth compared with milk.

READY FOR MORE
During her first few months your baby will change dramatically, not least in making the leap from a milk-only diet to eating solids.

Questions & Answers

Members of my family suffer from asthma and eczema. Does this affect when I give my baby solids?
Your baby is more likely to be prone to allergies if they already exist in the family, so it's best to be cautious. Waiting until your baby is at least six months old before introducing solids can help prevent allergies occurring.

How are allergies caused?
While your baby is young, her gut is more porous, so proteins (the parts of food that cause allergies) can leak into the bloodstream. Your baby's immune system reacts to these proteins in the way it would react to germs. Then, whenever she eats that particular food, her immune system reacts as if it is an infection. She has what is called an "allergic reaction".

Why does it help to wait until six months before introducing solids?
The older your baby is when she first tastes real food, the more mature her digestive system has become. The proteins are less likely to leak into the bloodstream and your baby can handle different foods without having an allergic reaction. Also, her immune system is more mature and better at recognizing the difference between a food protein and bacteria. Exclusively breastfeeding until your baby is six months old may not prevent her developing an allergy, but it can reduce the likelihood and severity. In babies who have no solids before six months, allergies appear later, tend to be milder and the children grow out of them earlier.

6-9
months

"With each **new skill** that she acquires, Emma's becoming so much more independent."

LOUISE, mother of seven-month-old Emma

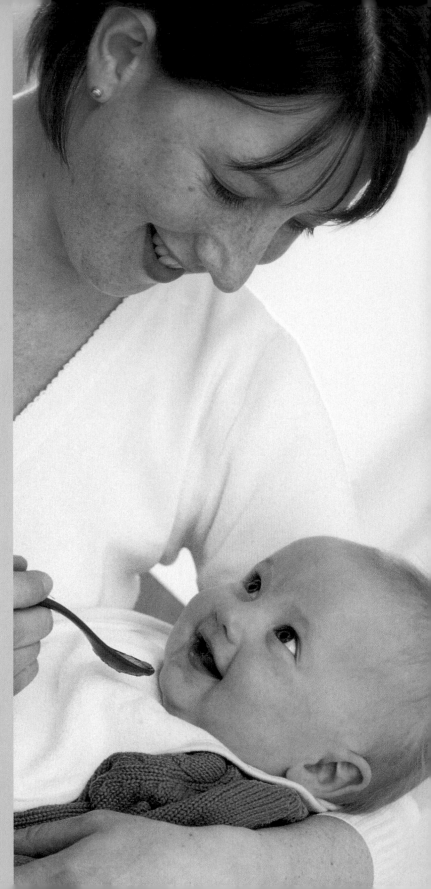

" I'll **never forget** the first time I gave James baby rice cereal – my husband took a **memorable photo** of him smiling at me as he had his first taste of solid food. **"**

RUTH, mother of six-month-old James

Feeding your baby

Giving your baby his first taste of solid food is an exciting moment. But his first tastes are more about experiencing something new rather than gaining extra nourishment. Being prepared – knowing which foods to serve, and what to expect – will help the moment go smoothly. Here we look at what you will need and how you can make your baby's first experience of solid food a happy one.

Be prepared

Your baby's first taste of food is a major milestone in his development and one you need to be ready for. Once you decide that the time is approaching when you will introduce solids, it's worth preparing for the big moment so you can feel calm and in control as you offer your baby his first mouthfuls.

You'll need to make a trip to the supermarket to buy your first few items of baby food. But don't go overboard. Remember, at this stage you are just offering your baby his first tastes of solid food and it may be a while yet before he's on three meals a day.

What you will need

For preparing food you will need:
• a nylon chopping board (wooden boards can harbour germs)

• one of the following for puréeing food, depending on budget: a nylon or steel sieve and a plastic and nylon or stainless steel spoon; a mouli (hand-turned food mill); or a small hand-held electric blender or food processor
• a steamer – good for fast cooking to preserve nutrients
• plastic containers with airtight lids for storing food in the fridge
• ice-cube trays for freezing surplus food in convenient small portions
• freezer bags for storing frozen cubes of purée.

For serving food you will need:
• lots of soft fabric bibs (easy to wear and easy to wash) and a plastic bib with curved bottom designed for catching food (especially useful once your baby starts feeding himself)
• a set of plastic bowls – unbreakable and easy to wash

Where should my baby sit?

You can sit your baby on your lap or strap him into his baby seat or car seat, preferably placed on the floor for safety. If he still can't sit up unaided, he will need to be slightly reclined – but he should be sufficiently upright to eat and swallow without choking.

• plastic teaspoons with soft or rounded edges – easier on your baby's tender gums.

Great expectations

Lots of parents have a camera ready to record the moment when their baby has his first taste of solid food – but don't expect too much! Remember that this is the first time your baby has tasted anything other than milk.

The new taste and texture will probably baffle him and, chances are, what goes in – if anything does – will roll straight back out again!

As with all skills, learning to eat food takes time and practice. Your baby will go at his own pace, but there is much that you can do to encourage his interest in food.

• Let him sit on your lap at family meals so he can see everyone enjoying their food.

• As he becomes more adept at using his hands he'll love playing with food. Let him squish a piece of cooked pasta or dip his hands in some yogurt.

• Talk to him while you are preparing his food – whether you are getting ready to breastfeed, fixing a bottle or getting his solids ready.

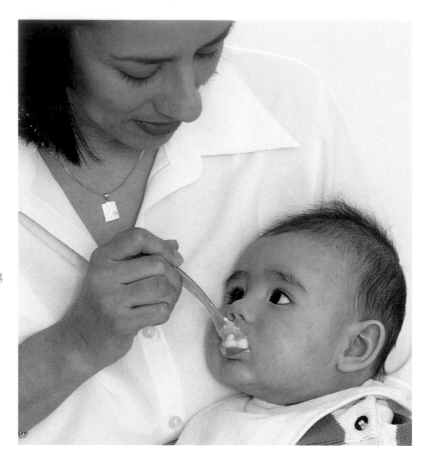

How to give the first feed

• Talking to your baby all the time, prepare a small amount of food using the methods described on page 92. Then give him up to half of his usual milk feed to take the edge off his appetite.

• Sit him on your lap or in a baby seat or car seat. Using a plastic spoon, place a tiny amount of food in between his lips. Don't push it in too far or your baby may gag. And don't worry if he pushes it straight back out – he'll soon learn how to suck food from the spoon. A tiny amount will stay put and you can scoop the remainder up and slip it back in.

• Give your baby lots of loving attention – chat, smile, tell him how wonderful he is. Make a point of touching him and stroking him whenever you can to help him feel safe and secure.

• Try another spoonful, but don't expect him to take more than a couple of tiny teaspoons. Don't worry if most of it ends up smeared around his face – he's discovering what it feels like and is more likely to let you try again if he is having fun.

• Once your baby has had enough he'll turn his head away, close his mouth or lean back.

• Tell him how clever he is and give him lots of cuddles. Finish up with the remainder of his milk feed if he's interested.

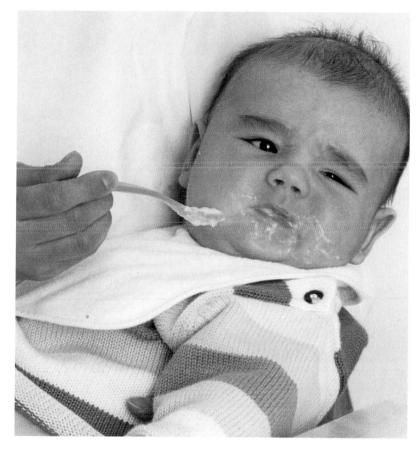

Expert tip

It's not unusual for a baby to gag if he is offered a food he doesn't recognize, too large a mouthful or a texture that's slightly thicker than normal. Gagging is a protective reflex – it helps get the food back to the front of the mouth where it can be spat out or repositioned. Try thinning first foods a little more if your baby gags. All food, however, can cause choking, so it's vital never to leave your baby alone while he has food or drink in his mouth. Talk to your health visitor if gagging or choking become a regular occurrence.

A WHOLE NEW EXPERIENCE
Give your baby tiny amounts of food at a time to begin with. When he has had enough he will close his mouth and turn his head away.

Tell him what you are doing and praise him for watching. He'll love your attention and learn to associate mealtimes with happy occasions.

A new skill to learn

Once you've decided that today is the day for giving your baby a taste of something new, get everything ready beforehand and choose a time when you are both feeling happy and relaxed. Introducing new foods takes time, so it may be worth putting on the answering machine and forgetting about other chores while you give your baby your full attention.

Most babies screw up their faces with surprise no matter how much they like the new tastes. So how do you know whether your baby loves or loathes the food you are giving him?
● If he likes it he'll open his mouth for more, in which case you can continue to offer him a few teaspoons each day, gradually increasing the thickness of the purées.
● If he doesn't like it he'll turn his head away, cry or won't seem interested. Don't worry – chances are today is just not the day. Try again tomorrow. If your baby still isn't keen, wait a few days before giving it another go. If he still isn't keen talk to your health visitor.

Don't be worried if your baby is finding it hard to get the hang of eating solid food – until now he has always taken his food by sucking, and learning how to feed from a spoon needs lots of practice. His tongue-thrust reflex (see page 79) is only just starting to disappear and

Trying new tastes

Some babies are naturally reluctant to try new tastes. Here are some ideas to help you both.

● Serve your baby's food at either room temperature or slightly warmed.

● If your baby rejects the spoon, dip a clean finger into the food and let him suck the food off it.

● Try offering some food after a shorter breast- or bottle-feed than usual. If he's alert but not over-hungry he may be keener.

● Don't make up too much – ready-to-mix baby cereal rather than ready-mixed gives you the option of using tiny quantities.

often the food you give your baby will simply dribble out because he doesn't know how to get it far enough back on his tongue to swallow.

Give him only a tiny bit of food, holding the spoon close to his lips. If he likes what he tastes he'll soon discover that by sucking he can draw the food off the spoon. Sucking will also help him get the food to the back of his mouth so he can swallow it.

When your baby has had enough, he'll close his mouth or turn his head away. However much is left in his bowl, don't force him to take any more – your baby needs to decide for himself whether he's still hungry and which foods he likes. And while,

at this stage, it's hard to tell whether he's rejecting a new taste because he doesn't like it or is still mastering the art of eating, it's better to be cautious than pushy.

What to avoid

Never add any of the following to your baby's food:

● salt – this can overload his kidneys

● sugar – this can encourage a sweet tooth

● honey in liquid or solid form – it can contain spores that cause infant botulism: the digestive systems of babies under one year old are immature, and spores can germinate and cause disease.

DAD'S TURN
Starting on solids provides a great opportunity for dad to get involved with feeding.

PASTA PLAY
Allowing your baby to handle solid food will help him explore and get used to different shapes and textures.

Don't be tempted to mix baby rice into your baby's bottle. Adding cereal to bottles risks over-feeding your baby and can cause choking. Also, it's important that your baby gets used to the mechanics of eating: taking a spoonful, resting, taking another and stopping when he's full. Experiencing first foods in this way will help your child develop good eating habits which will last him a lifetime.

Nappy changes

Once you start introducing solids you will notice the consistency and colour of your baby's stools changes. They will be more solid, darker and probably smellier! This may come as a bit of a shock – especially if up until now your baby has been totally breastfed and his nappies fairly inoffensive. The change is perfectly normal. His digestive system is still immature and the food often doesn't change much in between going in and coming out again.

If your baby's stools become hard, you notice him straining, or there is a reduction in the number of his stools each day, talk to your health visitor as your baby may be constipated.

Questions & Answers

When's the best time of day to give my baby his first foods?
Your baby needs to be relaxed, not too hungry and not too tired. Early morning and late evening may not be the best times as your baby might be hungry, half awake or half asleep. He may be more cooperative mid-morning and late afternoon. Watch him closely and feed him when he's happy, hasn't had a milk feed for a while, yet isn't too hungry.

Will starting my baby on solid food help him to sleep through the night?
Lots of parents imagine that introducing their babies to solids will help them sleep through the night. Research shows that this isn't the case. Babies routinely wake in the night – even when they are not hungry – and until they learn how to comfort themselves and fall back to sleep on their own, they are unable to sleep for extended periods of time.

My baby just isn't interested in solids. What should I do?
It's much more important at this stage that both of you enjoy mealtimes, and if, despite your best efforts, your baby isn't keen to give solids a go, don't force the issue. Instead, go back to breast- or bottle-feeding exclusively for a few days and then try again. If you have concerns, talk to your health visitor.

How should I prepare my baby's food?

Preparing simple purées made from fruit and vegetables for your baby needn't take long – and it's less expensive than shop-bought baby food. With a few simple precautions and cooking tips you can give your baby safe and healthy meals. You can also easily prepare small quantities in advance so they are ready to hand when your baby needs to be fed.

Making your own purées

Try to cook fresh fruit and vegetables within a day or so of buying them.

1 Wash and prepare the fruit or vegetable and cut into even-sized pieces.

2 Steam or boil (use as little water as possible to preserve the nutrients).

3 When soft, allow the food to cool a little then purée using a mouli (hand mill), food processor or hand-held blender. Alternatively, you can push it through a sieve.

4 Test the temperature of the food on your fingertip or arm before giving it to your baby – room temperature or slightly warm is best. Babies' palates are very sensitive, so be careful not to burn your baby's mouth.

HEALTHY COOKING
Using a steamer to cook your baby's food will help preserve the nutrients which are normally lost during the cooking process.

PUREEING YOUR BABY'S FOOD
A hand-operated food mill is ideal for puréeing your baby's cooked food. This stage won't last for long so don't buy an electric blender or liquidizer specifically for this purpose.

PREPARE IN ADVANCE
You can have home-cooked baby food always on hand if you make a large quantity of purée in advance, and freeze spoonfuls of it in a sterilized ice-cube tray.

Freezing and storing

At this stage your baby is only tasting a tiny amount of food. Unused purée can be spooned into a sterilized ice-cube tray and frozen until needed. You can also freeze ahead – make a large amount of purée, spoon it into a sterilized ice-cube tray and freeze until the cubes are solid. Turn the cubes into a plastic bag, seal and label before returning to the freezer. Individual cubes can then be removed and defrosted in the fridge in a bowl or on a plate. Heat through as and when required.

You can sterilize a freshly washed ice-cube tray by washing it in the dishwasher or putting it in a pan of boiling water for five to 10 minutes.

Food hygiene

Food poisoning is easy to prevent. Make eating safe for your baby by taking the following precautions:

★ wash your hands carefully before feeding your baby – especially if you have been handling raw food

NUTRITION AT THE READY
When frozen, turn the cubes of puréed food out of the tray and store in sealed freezer bags, one type of food per bag. Carefully label and date each bag and use within three months of freezing.

★ keep kitchen equipment and work spaces as clean as possible

★ don't save leftovers from the bowl your baby has just used – bacteria will grow and any enzymes from your baby's saliva will thin the food out

★ if you are using a ready-made jar of food, remove as much as you need rather than feeding directly from the jar, unless you are finishing the jar off

★ if you are heating your baby's food, heat only enough for one meal and discard any leftovers

★ keep food cold in the fridge for up to 24 hours and use warm food as soon as it's ready.

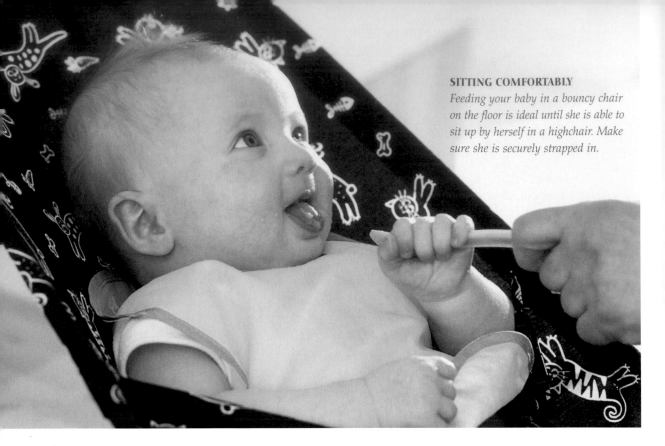

" I prepare Daniel's purée before giving him a breastfeed. He loves sitting in his chair watching me. I'm sure he's finishing on the breast quicker so he can get to his solid food sooner!"

SIMONE is mum to Daniel, six months

Some time around her six-month birthday you can give your baby her first taste of solid food. If she likes it you can build up to two or three mini-meals a day. Over the next few weeks you can start introducing a wider variety, but it's important to take your time, and watch out for allergic reactions.

Once she is eating two or three spoonfuls of baby cereal or a home-made purée every day, try a different single food. Don't be worried if she doesn't accept it straight away. It's perfectly normal to have to offer a new food between 10 and 20 times before it's accepted. Once your baby clearly likes the taste, give this new food exclusively for at least a couple of days before trying another.

Offering one food at a time, and only one new food every two or three days, means that your baby can get used to each new taste and texture. It also means that, if there are any signs of an allergic reaction – such as tummy ache, diarrhoea or rashes – you will more readily identify which food was the culprit.

First purées to try include carrot, parsnip, swede, sweet potato, cooked apple, cooked pear and mashed banana. Once your baby is happy taking semi-liquid food from a spoon, gradually start to thicken the purée or cereal by adding less liquid.

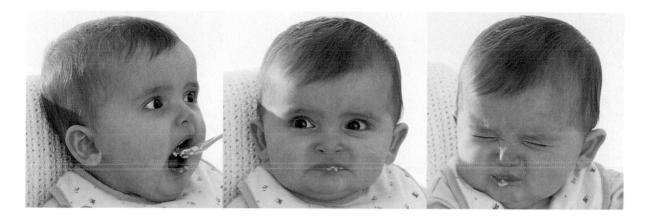

This allows your baby to practise her chewing and swallowing skills and will help ease the transition from purées to lumpier food.

If your baby has a reaction

Although some foods are more likely than others to cause problems, any food can potentially trigger an allergic reaction. Food allergies that affect the immune system are rare, but some children find certain foods more difficult to tolerate than others and may have a reaction.

If you think your baby had a reaction to a particular food, wait a couple of weeks before trying it again. The same reaction two or three times would suggest that your baby is sensitive and you should wait a few months before re-introducing it. See your health visitor if you are unsure.

Food combinations

Once your baby has taken several single foods with no adverse reaction, you can start mixing two foods together. Don't try mixing one food your baby loves with another she hates, as she may end up hating both. Combinations that work well at this age include broccoli and sweet potato, carrot and parsnip, and stewed apple and pear.

Milk needs at six months

Once your baby is happily taking two or three solid "meals" a day (although these meals may consist of only a couple of spoonfuls at each serving) with milk in between, you may find that she's not feeding as much from the breast or bottle. Usually, the early morning and pre-bedtime feed stay the same, but during the day your baby may nurse a little less or take a little less formula.

● **Good for nutrition** Although your baby is starting to eat real food, milk is still an essential part of her diet. Purées offer little in the way of extra calories – and calories are what your baby needs to maintain her growth and weight gain. Until she's on three proper meals a day, she still needs around 600ml (20fl oz) of milk a day. If you are breastfeeding it's impossible to check, but if you let your baby take the lead chances are she's taking what she needs. If you have concerns, talk to your health visitor.

● **Good for comfort** Although your baby is starting to recognize that solids can satisfy hunger as well as milk, sucking is still a way of feeling close to you. Your baby loves nothing better than feeling safe and secure in your arms, and breastfeeding or bottle-feeding her is still important as a way of giving her comfort.

What is gluten?

Gluten is a protein that's found in wheat, barley, rye and perhaps oats. Sensitivity to gluten can trigger coeliac disease. In a small number of babies, when the intestine comes into contact with gluten an allergic reaction occurs in its lining. The lining becomes smooth, preventing nutrients from being properly absorbed, and this is associated with a permanent intolerance to gluten. Symptoms include tummy pain, diarrhoea, weight loss, irritability and nausea.

Foods that contain gluten, such as bread, pasta and rusks, should never be given to babies under six months. Once your baby is six months old, her gut is more mature and less susceptible to developing gluten intolerance.

If coeliac disease is diagnosed, your child will need to eat a gluten-free diet for life. She'll be referred to a dietician who can advise you as to what she can and can't eat. Nowadays, larger supermarkets stock gluten-free alternatives, including bread, biscuits, cereals and pasta.

WATCH AND LEARN
Open your mouth as you offer your baby her food, and she will probably open hers in response.

Shop-bought baby food

There are lots of advantages to making your own baby food – it's cheap, easy and your baby can get used to the types of food your family normally eats. But there are times when ready-made jars are more convenient – when you are travelling is a good example. You can choose from lots of different flavours and ingredients and they are usually categorized according to age. They don't contain salt but some do have added sugar and modified starch, so it's worth reading the list of ingredients carefully. Always remember to: check the use-by date on the container; store unopened jars in a cool place; make sure the vacuum seal button is down — don't use a jar if the seal has popped up; don't feed from the jar – take the amount of food your baby needs out of the jar and serve separately; once opened, keep the jar with its remaining contents in the fridge – it should stay fresh for one to two days, but always read the label.

Are organic fruit and vegetables best?

Many people are worried about the effects on children's health of pesticides and other chemicals used to produce food. Organic fruit and vegetables are grown in soil fertilized with manure and compost rather than synthetic chemicals. Research has shown that levels of pesticides in non-organic produce such as fruit and vegetables are typically well below the safety levels set by government agencies. You can take extra care with your child's health by washing fruit and vegetables thoroughly before cooking and serving.

Foods to avoid at six months

Advice on which foods are suitable for your baby can sometimes change, so check also with a health visitor or at your baby clinic. But as a general guideline you should not give the following foods to babies who are six months old:

- **nuts and nut products**, especially those containing peanuts: for babies with a family history of allergies continue to avoid these up to the age of three; whole nuts should not be given to children until age seven or older because of the risk of choking

- **foods that carry a higher risk of food poisoning** such as mould-ripened cheeses, liver pâté and soft-boiled eggs (up to the age of nine months only yolk should be given as this is the high-nutrition part of an egg, and whites are more likely to cause allergies)

- **salt**: your baby's kidneys are too immature to cope with this

- **sugar, honey or other sweeteners**: can lead to a sweet tooth and honey can also contain a potentially dangerous spore (see page 90) – if you need to, sweeten desserts with mashed banana

- **soft drinks**: may contain high levels of artificial sweeteners; offer cooled, boiled water or occasionally diluted unsweetened fruit juice at mealtimes if you want to give your baby an alternative to milk

- **tea**: can reduce iron absorption

- **low-fat and high-fibre foods**: babies need more calories and less bulk to give them the energy they need to grow

- **processed foods**: these contain too much salt.

Every baby is different

Your baby may take a couple of weeks to get the hang of solids. This is fine, as long as she is drinking plenty of milk to meet her nutritional needs. On the other hand, your baby may race ahead and manage two or three "meals" a day in no time at all. If your baby is happily eating solids, coping well with taking food from a spoon, and enjoying a wide range of fruit and vegetable purées, you may wish gradually to start introducing other foods, such as meat, poultry, lentils or split peas, to her purées.

Remember that your baby's digestive system is still adjusting to solid food, so add only small quantities of new foods – and still just one at a time in case she has an allergic reaction. You may find it takes longer for your baby to accept meat and poultry, so purée a tiny amount with her favourite vegetable.

When is the best time to start giving my baby finger foods?

Every day your baby is getting better at using his hands and fingers and this makes it easier for him to do things such as trying to feed himself. His hand-eye coordination is coming on in leaps and bounds, and now he can pick up a piece of food and then put it into his mouth - although not without a bit of mess!

"I CAN HOLD IT"
Your baby will be triumphant as she masters the ability to pick up pieces of food herself and put them in her mouth.

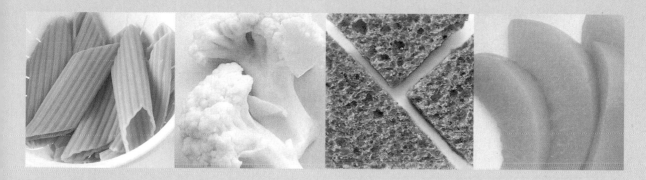

Getting started

Most babies are ready for finger food by about seven months. For a while yet, your baby will hold the food in his fist and work hard to push in the last mouthful using the flat of his hand. Over the next few months, however, he'll start to pick up things using his thumb and forefinger, a skill called the pincer grasp. In time this will allow him to pick up tiny pieces of food such as raisins or peas.

Your baby can easily choke by eating too fast or putting too much into his mouth. Stay close – and never leave your baby alone at mealtimes.

Learning to chew

Practising chewing is important not just because it means your baby can eat a wider range of food. Chewing also helps your baby practise moving his mouth and tongue, ready to learn how to talk. Your baby is using his gums to chew so choose

foods that can be gummed to a soft consistency for swallowing or those that will dissolve in his mouth without chewing. Here are some ideas:

★ cubes of bread, rice cakes and toast
★ dry cereals
★ chunks of soft fruit such as banana or melon
★ small pieces of cooked vegetable such as carrot, broccoli and cauliflower
★ well-cooked pasta, cut down in size if necessary
★ tiny cubes of hard cheese.

PREPARING FINGER FOOD

Even if your baby has some teeth he'll still use his gums to chew for a while yet. Always cut food into manageable chunks and don't offer him too much at a time. He might just try and stuff it all in at once – or sweep the lot on to the floor!

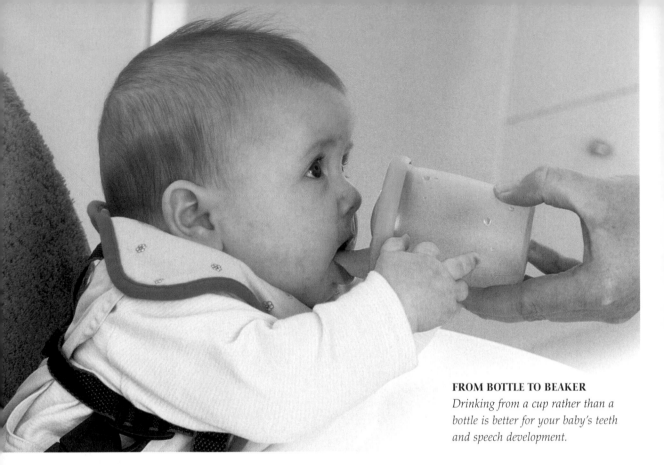

FROM BOTTLE TO BEAKER
Drinking from a cup rather than a bottle is better for your baby's teeth and speech development.

Foods to avoid at seven to nine months

At this age there are still certain foods that are not suitable for your baby. Continue to avoid:

● **adding salt, sugar and honey**: use mashed banana for sweetening desserts instead

● **nuts**: avoid all nuts and nut products, especially if your family is known to have a history of allergies

● **foods that present a choking hazard**: these include whole grapes, nuts, large pieces of apple or raw carrot, uncooked peas and celery

● **soft drinks**: may contain high levels of artificial sweeteners; offer cooled, boiled water and occasionally diluted fruit juice at mealtimes if you want an alternative to milk

● **foods that carry a higher risk of food poisoning** such as mould-ripened cheeses, liver pâté and soft-boiled eggs (up to the age of nine months only yolk should be given as this is the high-nutrition part of an egg, and whites are more likely to cause allergies)

● **low-fat and high-fibre foods**: babies need more calories and less bulk to give them the energy they need to grow

● **processed foods**: these contain too much salt.

Seven to nine months

As the number of foods you can give your baby rapidly expands, mealtimes will become easier as he starts to enjoy some of the same foods as everyone else. Over the next few months your baby will be building up to three regular meals a day with two or three snacks in between. He'll now be sitting up on his own for extended periods and will be keen to get more involved in feeding himself. Letting him have a spoon of his own will encourage him – as will offering him finger foods. You can start introducing lumpier food so he can develop his chewing skills.

Calories

Your baby still needs lots of calories every day for energy and growth. Introducing a wider variety of food into his diet helps a lot. But to make sure your baby is getting enough protein, calcium and vitamins at around seven to nine months, whatever else he eats he still needs about 500–600ml (17–20fl oz) of formula or two full breastfeeds every day.

Advancing to a cup

Your baby will naturally feel thirsty while he's eating. This is a good time to introduce a beaker or cup so he can take sips of water or fruit juice during mealtimes. Limit the amount of juice he drinks to 120ml (4fl oz) a day and dilute it at least one part juice to three parts water.

- Choose a non-drip, soft-spout cup for first-timers. Some babies prefer a cup with one or two handles, others prefer no handle.
- Help by holding the cup to your baby's mouth and tipping it for him to show him how it works.
- Expect your baby to play with it at first. It may well be waved around and thrown from the highchair (and this is all part of the learning process).
- Avoid letting him carry it around with him – offer it to him only while he is in his highchair.

Foods your baby can eat

Your baby is now ready for a whole range of tastes and can share many of your family meals – provided no sugar or salt has been added. Remember to introduce new tastes and textures gradually.

Try to include at least one protein-based meal a day – fish, meat, egg yolks, lentils or beans – as these are good sources of protein and iron. Iron is particularly important as by the time your baby is six months old the iron stores with which he was born are starting to dwindle and milk alone will not satisfy all his daily requirements (see page 79).

Make sure your baby also has a portion of fruit, vegetables and starchy food every day, too. He can also eat foods containing gluten, so try white or wholemeal bread, pasta or couscous.

And you can now use cows' milk in meals – added to cereal, for example.

Protein
- beans and pulses
- cheese
- chicken/turkey
- cows' milk in meals (e.g. with cereal)
- eggs (yolks only, as their nutritional value is higher and they are less likely to cause allergies than whites)
- boneless fish
- red meat
- tofu

Fruit
- grapes (cut in half and pips removed)
- orange (seedless)
- mango
- melon
- satsuma
- strawberries
- pieces of pear

Vegetables
- butternut squash
- cucumber
- green beans
- leek
- peas
- mushroom
- onion
- sweetcorn

Starchy food
- potatoes
- bread
- noodles
- rice
- pasta
- couscous
- breakfast cereals
- porridge

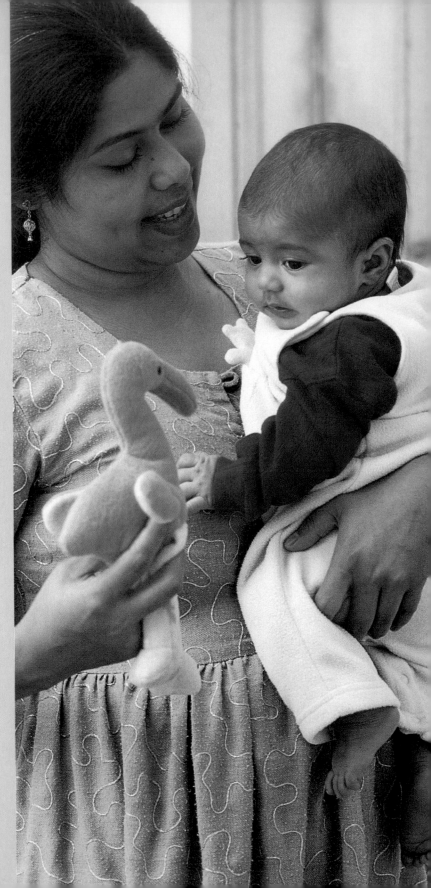

" Natasha doesn't like being left alone – that always makes her cry. I **comfort her** by picking her up and rubbing her back, and saying, **'It's okay.'** Then I find something to amuse her. "

JENNIFER, mother of six-month-old Natasha

Crying in older babies

From around three to six months of age, your baby will begin to cry less. Even those babies who have cried excessively should have shown signs of settling down by six months. You're more confident because you are more in tune with your baby, and have many effective ways of soothing her.

A turning point

Many babies do just grow out of crying excessively, often by around three months. This is partly related to your baby's development – she's now becoming more sociable and is able to do more, such as grasp a toy or roll over.

It is also because your older baby is more adept at finding ways of soothing herself, such as being able to find her own thumb to suck or becoming attached to a "transitional" comfort object.

It is true that a few babies who did not seem to cry excessively in the early days begin to cry more around five to six months. This may be caused by teething or distress at the introduction of solid foods. It is also a possibility that they need to cry more to ensure more interaction with their parents, who may have been providing them with less attention because they had seemed so much more settled! Either way, you have learned so much over these last months about handling your baby, finding out her likes and dislikes, that you now deal easily with her needs. You have a better understanding of the different patterns of her crying. You will probably have many effective ways of comforting her.

More good news!

By now, family life is settling into a more comfortable routine. You know how you can keep her happy a lot more of the time, and it's rewarding when she takes an interest in toys, or watches you contentedly from a sitting position while you carry out jobs around the house. This in turn means that there is a much wider range of activities you can try to calm her when she does cry.

Checklist

All babies cry less after three months. This is partly developmental, but also it is because:

- she's taking an interest in the world around her, so there's more to see and do

- she's more active and is busy developing her motor skills

- she's more sociable and is better able to interact with you and other caregivers

- you know your baby well by now and can recognize her crying triggers

- you have more effective ways of soothing her crying.

Why older babies cry

Hunger, over-stimulation and overtiredness are still likely causes for your older baby's crying. You will probably be familiar with the signs to look out for now and be ready to comfort her.

However, there are now a number of new reasons why your older baby cries.

• Crying for attention

Older babies can cry intentionally, because they want you to come to them, and then act pleased to see you. It is wrong to think of this as "naughty" or your baby manipulating you. She still uses crying as a means of communicating her needs and emotions. Also, there is no one in the world as important to your baby as you. She wants to spend time with you, and demonstrates this by squealing with delight whenever you come to her. This is part of the magic of parenting.

• Starting solid foods

You may notice more crying at mealtimes when your baby is trying her first solids from around six months. This could be because your baby simply dislikes the new feeding experience, or the taste of the food. She may reject a cup or spoon, or object to having to wait for her milk after her meal.

• Boredom

The chances of your baby feeling bored can increase as she grows older and spends less time sleeping during the day, so that bouncers, toys, mobiles and your company all become increasingly important because they help to keep her occupied for parts of the day.

• Anxiety and fright

Your older baby may start to worry about things that never bothered her before. Typically, it may be the sound of the vacuum cleaner, or the sight of an animal, or having her hair washed that starts the crying.

Even if these fears seem trivial to you, you must not let her know that.

Teething

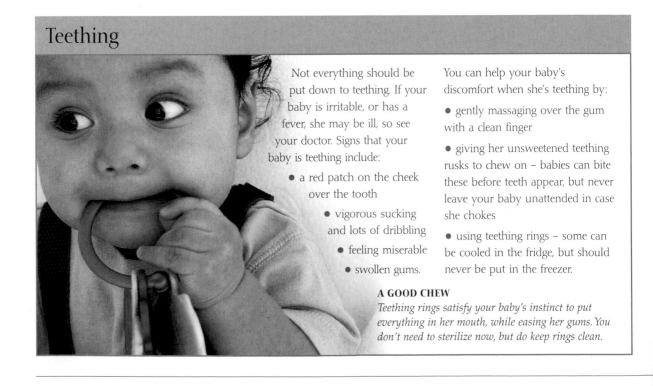

Not everything should be put down to teething. If your baby is irritable, or has a fever, she may be ill, so see your doctor. Signs that your baby is teething include:

- a red patch on the cheek over the tooth
- vigorous sucking and lots of dribbling
- feeling miserable
- swollen gums.

You can help your baby's discomfort when she's teething by:

- gently massaging over the gum with a clean finger
- giving her unsweetened teething rusks to chew on – babies can bite these before teeth appear, but never leave your baby unattended in case she chokes
- using teething rings – some can be cooled in the fridge, but should never be put in the freezer.

A GOOD CHEW
Teething rings satisfy your baby's instinct to put everything in her mouth, while easing her gums. You don't need to sterilize now, but do keep rings clean.

Separation anxiety

Having spent all the early months of her life becoming attached to you, it is very common for your baby not to want to let you out of her sight from about seven to eight months. Often this new behaviour coincides with the time when you need to introduce childcare for the first time, perhaps because you are returning to work.

Some babies will be more "clingy" than others, considering everyone other than Mummy or Daddy to be a "stranger" – even grandparents. Be patient with this phase. You are the centre of her universe, and she doesn't yet understand the concept of time, or know that when you leave her, you will definitely be coming back.

Your baby needs plenty of loving sympathy, as these fears seem very real to her.

● **Loss of a comforter**
Your baby may have become very attached to a security object, such as a dummy, a soft toy or even a scrap of cloth. It can cause great distress and crying if it gets lost or mislaid, most often in her cot during the night.

Make sure you have a spare one in case the precious original is lost for good, and always remember to take the comforter with you whenever you are out or staying away from home.

● **Frustration**
As your baby grows, she inevitably wants to try to do more, such as attempting to crawl before she's quite ready to or grab an interesting-looking toy that's just out of her reach, and is likely to cry when she realizes that she can't manage to do everything – or have everything – that she wants! She needs lots of help and comfort from you to prevent this frustration becoming overwhelming for her.

● **Bumps and bruises**
Once on the move, babies can hurt themselves in lots of ways that don't happen to younger babies, and the

Expert tips

The following will help your baby to cope with separation anxiety.

● Chat to her whenever you're out of sight – "Here I am, I'll be back soon" – or sing a song, so that she knows you're still there.

● Use games, such as peekaboo (popping out from behind the door, or even just covering your face with your hands). You are teaching her "object permanence", that a person can go and come back, and is still there even though she can't be seen.

● Move her to wherever you are if possible, and let her watch you – she will come through this phase sooner if she is not left alone feeling anxious.

● When you must leave a room briefly, try to involve her in an activity before you go.

● Set aside times to give her your undivided loving attention – cuddling up with a storybook or playing a game – as this helps security grow.

● If you have to leave her with another carer, such as a childminder or at daycare, take it slowly, allowing time for her to get used to the idea. Never sneak away, as this will upset her more. For sensitive children, even a short separation may need extra effort – explaining in advance, allowing lots of time for the handover, reassuring her that you will be back.

● Give your child something of yours that has your smell on it – a T-shirt, for example.

Questions & Answers

What are nightmares and night terrors?

Many children have nightmares, but a few may wake up crying from them. They happen in the lighter, dreaming (REM) phase of sleep, and older children can usually remember them in the morning. Reassure your baby and settle her back to sleep.

Night terrors are less common. They occur during deep sleep, and are not remembered on waking. They can be frightening for parents to witness. Your baby may be screaming, and thrashing around, but she will not be awake, so doesn't know what is happening. It is often better not to attempt to wake her up, but to try to gently soothe, perhaps whispering, "It's OK, I'm here. Don't be scared", and stroking gently.

If your baby's night terrors really worry you, try to spot a pattern. If they happen, for example, three hours after your baby goes to sleep, try to rouse her shortly before that time. Hopefully, you'll be able to settle her back to sleep again and intercept the event. Your baby will grow out them, without any harmful or long-term effects.

resulting bumps and knocks can lead to more tears. Plan ahead to childproof your home as your baby becomes more mobile. As well as protecting her from accidents, it can save frustration in the early years. Babies and toddlers do not have the ability to remember the word "No!" and repeating it can sometimes reinforce bad behaviour. With the freedom to explore safely, you will avoid having to repeat it to her until she is old enough to understand.

- ### "Grizzling" and "fussing"

This type of crying is common in some older babies, while others may never do it. It can help to treat this

as your baby's "conversation" and chat back to her, saying for example, "You're probably feeling bored going around this shop" or "You don't like sitting in that car seat, do you?" Anything interesting to create a distraction – for example, giving her a set of keys to jangle – will keep her amused for a while.

- ### Night crying

By around the age of three months, most babies can sleep for five-hour stretches at night, but one-third of babies still wake at one year, so there is wide variation, and a lot of babies will still be waking and crying in the night (see page 108).

ON THE MOVE
Whether she's rolling, crawling or already up on her feet, your older baby is likely to cry more from frustration or as a result of bumps as she struggles to perfect her skills.

WHERE IS SHE?
Peekaboo is more than just a game – it's teaching your baby "object permanence", that someone she loves is still there even though she can't see her.

Settling herself to sleep

You may have already started establishing ways to teach your baby to settle herself to sleep (see pages 71–77). From four months, such routines become important both for daytime naps and at bedtime.

● At the age of four months, your baby will need two daytime naps of two to three hours each. By nine months, these will probably be reduced to one to two hours each. It's best to try to put her down for these naps while she's still awake and at roughly the same time each day.

● Continue keeping bedtimes peaceful. Set up a calm "winding down" period with a recognizable routine, such as a bath, song or bedtime story, so that your baby always knows that "sleep time" is coming up.

● Aim to put her down in her cot while she's drowsy but still awake, so that she learns how it feels to fall asleep on her own and develops her own self-soothing strategies. She's also less likely to wake in the night and cry, because her surroundings are familiar and she can go back to sleep by herself.

● Reconsider any comforting routines you have been using so far, such as giving her a dummy, or lying down with her or stroking her to settle her to sleep. From four months, your baby will expect these as part of her routine, and once firmly established, they will be hard to change.

New challenges

It's important to allow your baby plenty of time to adjust slowly to any changes to her routine, whether it's her first tastes of solid food or a new childcare arrangement. Despite her developing maturity, it is asking too much of your baby to expect her to happily accept major changes overnight without some protest.

You will avoid unnecessary tears if you are always sympathetic to your baby's fears. Give her plenty of cuddles and loving attention to help her deal with them. Many babies take a while to adjust to new situations, and your baby is likely to need patient understanding from you for some time to come.

Questions & Answers

My eight-month-old son had been sleeping through until about 6am for some time – I thought that was it! But for the last week or two he's started waking and crying at least twice during the night. Why is this?

It is quite common for a baby who had begun to show signs of sleeping through the night to start waking and crying again at around eight to nine months. Babies this age might be more easily disturbed because they're more aware of their surroundings, and they may also find it harder to drop back to sleep without you to help them. They may have become very attached to a particular method of going to sleep, whether that involves sucking a dummy, holding a toy, or being cuddled by you, so they then need this again when they wake at night – even several times a night. Help him to develop better sleep habits (see right) and see if you can settle him back into a good night-time routine in which he can fall back to sleep on his own.

Night waking

Up to about six months of age, your baby will probably wake during the night. She may still wake to be fed during the night, but beyond six months if she wakes it is more likely to be because she wants comfort or because something has disturbed her. Night waking can also be a sign of growth spurts – both physical and developmental.

Waking up in the dark and silence can make her puzzled and frightened, and if she is unable to settle herself back to sleep, she will start crying for you.

It's quite common from this age for babies who had been sleeping through for some time to start a phase of night waking again (see *Questions & Answers*, left).

We all stir from time to time during the night as we move between states of quiet and active (REM) sleep, but most of the time we're able simply to drift off to sleep again. Babies need to learn how to do this, and there are ways in which you can encourage your baby to develop good sleep habits.

● Resist going in to your baby at the first whimper. She may just be stirring and if you leave her a minute or two she may stop crying and settle on her own.

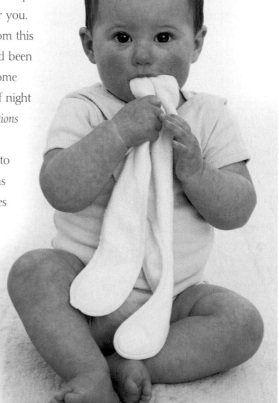

"Jack's cuddly blanket has a magical effect. He stops crying as soon as I hand it to him."

NEIL is dad to eight-month-old Jack

• You may want to try methods to encourage better sleep (see below), which are taught by some health professionals to parents to help manage their babies' crying and sleeplessness. The aim is to help your baby settle herself to sleep at bedtime and if she wakes at night.

• Try to avoid lifting her from the cot when she wakes (see below) but, if you have to, keep the room dark, speak quietly or rock her soothingly. You are aiming to help her understand that night-time is for sleeping, not for playing.

• If she regularly wakes at night, there could be something disturbing her. Check that she's not too hot or too cold and that her room is not too light or too dark. Consider also

whether she's being woken by a noise – perhaps she can hear you stirring if she's still sleeping in your room.

• Try to keep reminding yourself that these night-waking episodes are a very short time in a child's life. If you can deal patiently with your baby now, she will eventually feel secure in the knowledge that you or your partner will always come to her when you are needed, to answer calls of distress.

Encouraging better sleep

"Sleep training" can encourage your older baby to settle on her own, safe in the knowledge that you are there but understanding that her waking will not be rewarded with a cuddle or a feed.

Allow at least a week for it to start taking effect, and you may need to be prepared for things to get worse before they start getting better. Share the checking routine with your partner, if possible, but you both need to be consistent in your approach. Only try this when you are sure that your baby is not ill, hungry or in any form of discomfort.

You can encourage your baby to sleep in the following way.

• Adopt a "checking" routine – start by waiting for five minutes when she wakes crying before going in to her.

When you leave the room, she will probably continue to cry but wait for a minute longer than last time before going to check her again.

• Each time you go in to check her, keep the room dark, speak softly to her, stroke her, but don't pick her up. Firmly say goodnight and leave the room. It's important to stay calm – you will probably have to do this several times before your baby falls asleep.

• For babies who need you with them to settle down to sleep, try a gradual retreat, or "fading". Again, this works over several nights and involves you staying in the room with your baby until she falls asleep, but each night moving further away from her cot. Eventually, you will be outside the room when she falls asleep.

How can I comfort my older baby?

There are so many ways you can comfort your older baby. Toys and games are now a ready source of amusement to share with her if she's crying for your attention, while diversions and distractions work well when tears of frustration are threatening. And, of course, there will still be times when only a loving cuddle will do.

New ways to comfort her

★ **Toys** Choosing toys that are suitable for her stage of development will entertain your baby best. This is not just to ensure that the toy is safe for her to use, but also to avoid frustration if it's beyond her capabilities. Once she can grasp, she'll love rattles or musical toys. When she sits up, stacking cups and shape sorters will be fun. As soon as she's mobile, she'll enjoy anything she can push or pull. And nearer her first birthday, she'll be ready for simple puzzles.

★ **Laughter** Using humour will often avoid tears. Singing a song, such as "This is the way we wash our hands", can amuse your baby when routine tasks need to be done.

CUDDLE UP
You're still your baby's best comforter. She doesn't want to be apart from you at the moment, and a hug from you can make everything better, helping her feel secure, loved, and allaying her fears.

★ **Action rhymes** Songs and rhymes with actions to learn together, such as "Humpty Dumpty", "Pat-a-cake" or "The wheels on the bus", can be energetic and great fun. Games that lead to a tickle and a hug, such as "This little piggy" and "Round and round the garden", will soon become familiar to her and have her giggling in anticipation of the ending.

★ **Distractions and diversions** If you see trouble brewing, quickly try to turn your baby's attention to a new toy, or something that may be happening outside: "Oh listen, I think I can hear Daddy coming" or "Can you see a cat in the garden?" If she's playing with something you'd rather she didn't have, offer her an interesting alternative rather than simply taking it away.

MAKE MUSIC TOGETHER
Musical instruments are not just for singing along to. Your baby will learn "cause and effect", that by banging, shaking or blowing she can make a sound happen. Even some pans and a wooden spoon will do – if you can bear the noise!

SHARE A BOOK
It's never too soon to introduce your baby to books. She'll enjoy hearing you tell the story again and again and will point out familiar objects in the colourful pictures. Books that have different textures for her to feel and lift-the-flap stories add to her interest.

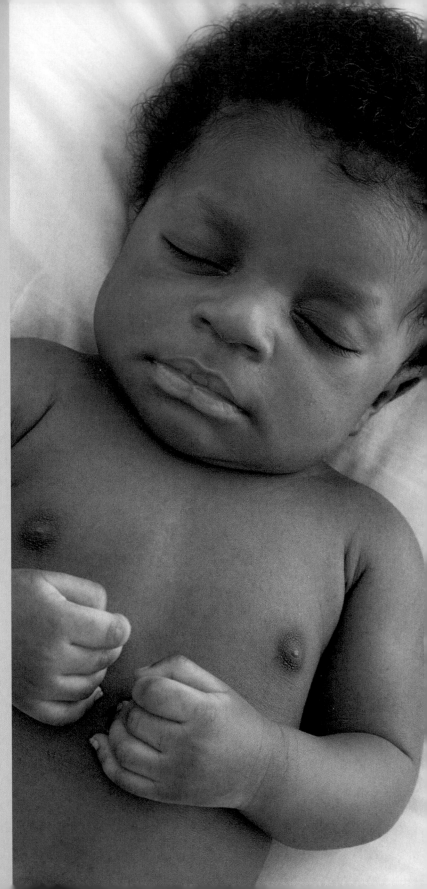

" Sonny's been so much **more settled** over the past few weeks – sometimes he'll go for five hours without waking. I love watching him as he sleeps. He looks like **an angel.** "

HANNAH, mother of six-month-old Sonny

Sleep routines

By the time your baby is six months old, his world will be an endless source of fascination, and he will be wide awake and alert during play periods. While he's more likely to sleep well after these interludes of intense activity, he may be less willing to cooperate at naptimes or bedtime – after all, there are so many interesting things to do. This is when you will reap the rewards of having a daytime and bedtime routine.

Longer nights

From six months, your baby will be able to sleep for longer periods at night. He'll probably spend around 11 hours asleep at night, although this is unlikely to be all in one uninterrupted stretch.

At this stage, most babies also take two regular daytime naps of an hour or more (one in the morning and one in the afternoon), but patterns will vary considerably.

Although many babies settle nicely into a healthy sleeping routine at this stage, many more will go through periods of disrupted night sleep.

Separation anxiety

At some point during the second half of his first year, your baby may suddenly start to become tense and fearful around strangers; he may cry when you leave the room or give him to someone else to hold (even someone familiar to him), and he may seem more clingy than usual. This is known as separation anxiety, and it is an important step forward in your baby's emotional development.

Separation anxiety is a healthy indication that your baby is slowly becoming aware of his independence from you, which is both exciting and frightening for him.

Your baby may suddenly become difficult to settle. He may get upset when you leave him to go to sleep, and bedtime and night-time awakenings may suddenly become complicated by problems that up until now hadn't bothered him. He may also be uncharacteristically frightened by loud noises or changes to routine, and he may start to wake at night and cry for you.

Checklist

There are several new reasons for night waking in babies aged from around six months.

• Your baby reaches many important developmental milestones during this period, and this may temporarily disrupt his sleep, particularly when he is acquiring his gross motor skills.

• Some connection between sleeping and eating remains, but the link is not as strong as it was. He no longer needs to feed at night, for example, so night feeds should be curtailed with your help (see page 114).

• Any changes to your baby's routine, for example a new childcare arrangement, illness or moving house, may temporarily disrupt sleep.

• Your baby now has a growing sense of being an individual, and may wake up and miss you in the night.

• He's now able to stay awake at will.

This is a normal and temporary phase, so stick to your routines as much as possible. Be extra loving and attentive towards your baby during the day, and keep night-time interactions with him supportive and caring, but brief and matter of fact.

It may be tempting to take him into bed with you as he goes through this phase, but you could be storing up trouble if you expect him to sleep in his own bed afterwards. Although you may have to go into his room more frequently during this period to reassure him with calming words or a gentle stroke, at other times he may settle if you simply call out to let him know you are near. A comforting or "transitional" object (see pages 118–19) may help him now.

SETTLING HER BACK TO SLEEP
Keep night-time interactions with your baby brief. Speak softly to her, perhaps stroke her hand, but don't pick her up.

Any changes to your baby's daily routine may lead to a period of increased waking during the night. One significant change that could happen around this time is your return to work. As well as missing you, your baby will be coping with a new childcare arrangement. If he goes to day nursery, he may have to adapt to a new nap routine and the extra stimulation of a busy environment.

You may want to keep your baby up for a while when you come home from work. You can prepare for this before you return to work by moving his bedtime back gradually. But, again, stick to his usual routine, and a bedtime of no later than 8.30pm.

Avoiding overtiredness

Until now, there wasn't much to keep your baby up at night. But with so many new discoveries to make, toys

Dropping night feeds

From around six months, your baby no longer needs to be fed during the night. He may drop his night feeds himself, but it's more likely that he will need your help. The best way of doing this is to progressively reduce the amount of milk he has during night feeds. Stopping suddenly is not advisable – although your baby wouldn't suffer nutritionally, he has learnt to wake up expecting to be fed. You need to re-train him so that he no longer associates waking up or falling asleep with feeding. The following is only a suggestion, but one that has worked for many parents.

● **If you are breastfeeding**, you can judge how much milk your baby is getting by the number of minutes he spends at the breast. Reduce this by a minute each night, and increase the periods between feeds by half an hour.

● **If bottle–feeding**, put 30ml (1fl oz) less in the bottle for night-time feeds. Decrease by the same amount every night, and increase the time between feeds by half an hour.

● **When your baby wakes up** and it's not time for a feed, comfort him, but don't hold him. Pat him or speak to him softly, then leave the room once he is calm.

● **Enlist the help of your partner.** If you are breastfeeding, your partner may have more success in settling your baby than you because your baby won't be agitated by the smell of your milk.

It may take several days, but if you persevere, your baby will learn that his night wakings will not be rewarded with a feed and should sleep through as a result.

to play with, and physical skills to perfect, your baby may not want to take time out to sleep.

Because his brain no longer simply "shuts down" when he's tired, he is able to stay awake even when he needs to sleep. Missing naps or going to bed late will make him irritable and may stop him from settling down, as well as make him more likely to wake during the night.

So, to prevent your baby becoming overtired, be consistent in your approach to his daytime naps and bedtime routines. Even if he doesn't seem tired, go through his usual calming bedtime rituals with him. Don't wait until he seems really tired before trying to settle him – putting him to bed calm and in a good mood is far more effective than if he's agitated and tearful.

CHECKING YOUR BABY
If you want to check that your baby's sleeping soundly during the night, always try to do so from the door of his room to avoid disturbing him if he's in a light stage of sleep.

Questions & Answers

My nine-month-old baby has suddenly dropped his morning nap. Is one daytime sleep enough for him?
Many babies drop one of their naps as they reach their first birthday, although others may continue to nap twice a day well into their second year. You'll know whether one nap a day is enough by your baby's mood. If he's irritable and overtired by lunchtime, it may be that he needs extra sleep but is fighting it because he's too excited by what's going on around him. Try putting him down straight after lunch. He will probably have a longer nap than usual – perhaps of around two hours – and this may become his only nap of the day.

" Often, Callum cries for me to stay as he falls asleep. To break the habit, each night I move further from his cot until I'm outside, and out of sight! "

EVE, mum to nine-month-old Callum

What is a good bedtime routine for my nine-month-old?

The benefits of having a well-established bedtime routine in place for your baby at this stage cannot be over-emphasized. If you're not sure what to include in your baby's bedtime routine, try some of the suggestions here. Experiment and see what works best for you and your baby.

Bedtime routines

A regular bedtime routine will:

★ give her the signals she needs that the day is over and that it's time to wind down and go to sleep

★ help to promote healthy and peaceful sleeping habits

★ give your baby a real sense of security

★ become an enjoyable and fulfilling part of your relationship for many years to come

★ help you to settle your baby after there's been some kind of disruption in her life, such as illness, a house move, or perhaps when staying away from home.

From now on, it's a good idea to feed your baby before you begin her bedtime routine. This will help

IT'S STORYTIME
Reading together is the perfect opportunity for a cuddle before bedtime, as well as encouraging in your baby a love of books.

her to dissociate sleeping and feeding, and it means she won't fall asleep at the breast or bottle. Learning to go to sleep without you is an invaluable skill. You could try some or all of the following in your baby's bedtime routine.

★ **Give her a bath** A bath is not just a way to keep your baby clean – it is warming and relaxing.

★ **Clean her teeth** Remember to do this every night after her last feed.

★ **Dim the lights** When it's time to put on her pyjamas or sleepsuit, draw the curtains in her bedroom, dim the lights and keep noise levels low. Any distractions should be kept to a minimum.

★ **Tell her a story** Settle down together and spend some quiet time looking at a book. Read to her, look at the pictures and let her explore the book and turn the pages if she likes.

★ **Give her a cuddle** A goodnight kiss and cuddle before you lift her into her cot ready for sleep will be a pleasurable end to the day for you both. Place your baby's favourite soft toy or blanket in her bed to help comfort her.

★ **Say goodnight** Once your baby is settled, leave the room. If she stirs or cries, wait a few minutes to see if she settles again. If she doesn't, go in to settle her, say goodnight again and leave.

CLEAN HER TEETH
Cleaning her teeth before bed is a useful sign that sleep time is near – and it teaches her good habits about looking after her teeth.

HAVE A BATH
With plenty of bath toys to amuse her, a bath is a fun and relaxing way to wind down before bed.

Getting ready for bed

Once you have established your baby's bedtime routine, it's worth building in some time beforehand to allow him to wind down from the day's activities.

It's a good idea to avoid boisterous activities and watching television in the hour or so before bedtime. Choose something soothing instead, such as looking at a book together. Other ways to ensure that your baby is ready to settle at bedtime include:

• avoiding giving him a heavy meal or a lot to drink before bedtime; a light snack or small drink is plenty

• not letting him fall asleep over his last feed, so that you can put him to bed awake but sleepy

• never leaving your baby with a bottle in his bed, as this can cause ear infections and tooth decay

• once you've put him down, avoiding rushing in to him at the first sound you hear, unless he really is in distress – if you leave him a few minutes he may settle down on his own.

Comfort objects

Between the ages of eight and 15 months, your baby may become attached to a certain object, such as a cuddly blanket or soft toy. These comforters are known as "transitional objects", and can help smooth the emotional passage from dependence to independence,

" Ella won't settle to sleep without her special blanket. She takes it with her to bed, and always looks for it during the day when she's tired or feeling unsure. I'm glad that she finds it such a comfort. "

CLAIRE is mum to nine-month-old Ella

especially when your baby is going through the developmental phase known as separation anxiety (see page 113). Having a comforting, familiar transitional object to snuggle up with or cling on to:

● reassures your baby when he's away from you

● helps him feel at home whenever he's in a strange place

● calms him down whenever he's feeling upset

● helps him relax into sleep.

Many parents find these comfort objects very helpful and actively encourage such an attachment, so that the chosen object becomes an indispensable companion for their child. You may want to keep a duplicate so that you can wash and dry one while the other is in use, and to be sure that you always have a replacement if the precious original is ever lost.

You will find that your baby will gradually give up his comfort object on his own as he finds more mature ways to deal with life's challenges.

For some babies, a dummy is a transitional object, but it's advisable to wean your baby off a dummy before he comes to rely on it as a part of his comforting routine.

Dummies at this stage can interfere with the development of your baby's language skills, may lead to more disturbed nights, and can be a difficult habit to break in later years (see page 59).

Questions & Answers

My seven-month-old bangs his head against the cot as he settles to sleep. Is this normal?
From around six months or so, a small percentage of babies and young children develop a habit of banging their heads against their cot bars or mattress, or indulge in some other repetitious, rhythmic activity, such as rocking themselves to sleep. While it may look alarming, this behaviour is not usually a sign that anything is wrong. It may last weeks, months or even years, but should have stopped by the age of three. If your baby is happy and isn't bruising himself, don't worry. But if head banging takes up a lot of his time, if he displays other unusual behaviour or is developing slowly, see your doctor.

Coping with teething

Teething is often blamed for night waking, but in many cases this is a false diagnosis. Your baby's first teeth will appear between five and 10 months, and this coincides with the onset of waking for other developmental reasons.

Symptoms of teething include mild irritability and dribbling. The gums around the emerging teeth may be swollen and tender, and he may want to bite on something firm, such as a teething ring, his fist or your finger. Talk to your doctor if your baby is clearly uncomfortable.

It's important not to blame teething every time your baby seems more unsettled than usual in case he is ill. A slightly raised temperature is normal when teething, but a temperature of 38°C (100.4°F) or more will not be caused by teething, and nor will diarrhoea or vomiting. In these cases, see your doctor.

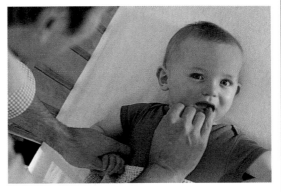

MAKING IT BETTER
Gently massaging your teething baby's gums with your fingertip can help to soothe his discomfort.

"Phoebe's always putting things in her mouth, especially **her toys**. I do wash them from time to time but, more regularly, I check for **broken bits** and throw the toys away if I find any."

KATE is mum to six-month-old Phoebe

Your baby's safety

Whether your child has just learned to roll over or begin to walk, each developmental milestone brings feelings of pride and fulfilment to you both. However, every new skill your child masters brings with it its own set of safety rules. So, throughout his early childhood, you will need to be one step ahead of him at all times to keep him safe.

The first (and easiest) thing you can do to safeguard your child is simply to look around your home. Sit on the floor for a child's eye view, and think about the things that are likely to attract his natural curiosity.

As your child grows, continue to see things from his perspective, and re-evaluate safety requirements. At the same time, teach him to become more aware of potential dangers, by explaining in simple terms when things can burn or hurt, for example.

Childproofing your home doesn't have to be complicated. Simply removing sharp items from your kitchen's floor-level cupboards, fitting safety locks and electrical socket covers, or securing any unsteady furniture means you are childproofing. Whatever measures you take, they should help make you – and your child – feel safer and more relaxed.

Fire safety

House fires are the biggest single cause of accidental death of children in the home, mostly as a result of smoke inhalation. Following recommended safety rules will significantly reduce the risk of this happening to you – and save lives.
- Fit smoke alarms.
- Don't smoke in your house. If you must, ensure cigarettes and matches are extinguished completely, and dispose of them safely. Keep matches and lighters out of your child's reach.
- Work out an escape plan for you and your family. Get advice from your local fire brigade.
- As soon as your child is old enough, tell him what to do if he discovers a fire or hears the alarm.
- Keep all doors shut at night.
- Keep a fire extinguisher in your kitchen. A fire blanket is handy, too.
- Repair old or worn electrical flexes and do not overload electrical sockets.

Expert tips

Infants, toddlers and pre-school children should never be given toys with the following:

- electrical parts – anything that needs plugging into the mains
- parts that could be pulled off and swallowed and/or fit into a child's nose or ear
- exposed wires and parts that can get hot
- lead paint or other toxic materials (use non-toxic paints and crayons)
- breakable parts
- sharp points or edges
- glass or thin parts
- springs or hinges that can pinch tiny fingers or get caught in hair.

Dealing with burns and scalds

Between the ages of six months and two years, your child is more likely to burn or scald himself than at any other time in his life. Acting fast can make a burn much less serious than it might be otherwise.

What to do

• No matter how small or large the burn, immediately flood the affected area with cold running water for at least 10 minutes. Keep the rest of your child's body warm.

• If clothes are not stuck to your child's skin around the burned area, remove them (cut them, if need be) but if anything is sticking to the burn, do not attempt to remove it.

• If the burn is large, severe or you are at all concerned, **call 999**.

• Cover the area with a sterile dressing or any non-fluffy material to keep out infection. Cling wrap can make a good temporary covering if nothing else is available. Never apply creams or lotions to the skin.

• Large burns should always be seen by a doctor, but even smaller

SOOTHING TREATMENT
Take some of the heat out of a burn by immediately holding it under cold running water for at least 10 minutes.

burns may need medical attention, especially if the skin blisters. Don't break blisters, as this can cause infection.

• If your child's clothes catch fire, drop him to the floor and roll him in a coat, blanket or rug. Don't try to remove his

clothes. Follow the first aid advice above and **call 999**. If the burn is electrical, switch off electricity at the mains before applying first aid.

• Hold chemical burns under cold water for 20 minutes and **call 999**.

• If a fire starts in your home, shut the door on it, leave the building, and call the fire brigade immediately.

Fireplaces and heaters

Any fire with an open flame should have a protective fireguard around it. Ideally, it should be fixed to the wall.

• Never leave your child unattended in a room with a burning open fire, even if it has a fireguard.
• Don't place anything on the guard.
• Keep all furniture at least 1m (3ft) away from an open fire.
• Never let your child see you throwing things onto the fire.

• Keep temperatures down on radiators to avoid burns, and teach your child that they are hot and must never be touched.

• If you use electric heaters, keep your child, and any furniture, well away from them. Never place a heater on any surface but the floor.

Kitchen safety

For a small child, the kitchen is the most dangerous place in the house. Ideally, you should keep your baby or child out of the kitchen at all times, but often this isn't practical. Aim at least to keep him out when you are cooking. Installing a stair gate at your kitchen door will help.

Cupboards and drawers

• Use safety catches to keep cupboards, drawers and doors off-limits to your child.

• Store cleaners, bleach, furniture polish, dishwasher soap and other dangerous products in a high cabinet, preferably lockable, out of sight. These substances are lethal and should never be left within reach.

• If you have no option but to store some items under the sink, buy safety locks that refasten automatically every time you close the cupboard.

• Never transfer toxic substances into containers that look as though they might hold food or drink.

• Keep knives, forks, scissors and other sharp instruments separate from safer kitchen utensils, and in a latched drawer.

• Store plastic bags in a drawer or cabinet with a safety catch.

OUT OF HARM'S WAY
The most effective way to protect your child from burns and scalds when you're cooking – and, most likely, distracted – is to keep her out of the kitchen.

Expert tips

The cooker is potentially the most dangerous kitchen appliance.

• Always turn pot handles towards the back of the stove.

• Whenever you're cooking or carrying hot food, keep your child out of the kitchen so you don't trip over him – a stair gate across the kitchen doorway is a good idea.

• When cooking, try to use the back burners only.

• If you have a gas stove, turn the dials firmly to the "off" position, and, if they're easy to remove, do so when you are not cooking.

• Install a cooker or oven guard.

• Teach your child that the oven is hot and not for touching, and keep reinforcing this message.

Aluminium foil and cling-wrap boxes can also be hazardous, as their serrated edges can cut little fingers.

● Unplug appliances on work counters when not in use, and keep cords out of your child's reach.

Household appliances

Fridges, freezers, washing machines and tumble driers could prove fatal if your child becomes trapped in one by climbing inside. If the door closes on them, tight-fitting seals will cut off the air supply, and a child's cries may go unheard. Warn your child of the dangers of playing inside an appliance, and keep all doors firmly closed after use. When discarding appliances, remove the doors first. There are safety factors worth noting with other household appliances.

Rubbish bins

These can make unwitting playgrounds. Young children enjoy nothing more than rooting around in search of interesting playthings.

● Keep your bin locked in a cupboard, if possible.

● When disposing of broken glass, always wrap it well in newspaper before placing it in the bin.

● Tie knots in plastic bags before throwing them away.

CUPBOARD LOCKS
Some safety locks fit inside a cupboard door, allowing you to open the door a little way before releasing the catch. These catches automatically lock themselves as you close the door.

● Keep your microwave switched off at the mains when it's not in use.

● Never use the microwave to warm baby bottles or food, as it heats things unevenly, leaving pockets hot enough to scald your child's mouth.

● When loading the dishwasher, always place cutlery in the appropriate tray, handle-side up, so that no sharp points or edges face upwards when the door is open.

● Always make sure that your dishwasher door is securely closed, unless you are loading or unloading the dishes. When the door is open, keep your child out of the way. As well as being a dangerous tripping hazard, he may be tempted to stand or sit on the open door, and an unanchored machine may tip over.

Stair gates

Once your child starts to crawl – and preferably beforehand – it's best to install stair gates at the top and bottom of your stairway.

● There are many types of stair gates on the market; if you are choosing one for the top of a stairway, make sure that it screws into the wall for extra strength. Stair gates that use pressure or suction are not recommended for use at the top of the stairs, as your child could push through them and fall. Accordion-style gates, which can trap arms or even necks, are also not recommended.

● Make sure the gap between any stair gate and the floor is less than 5cm (2in) wide.

● Leave the first two or three stairs at the bottom of your stairway free, so that your baby can practise climbing on them.

Windows

Falls make up a large proportion of injuries in children under five. The majority of these are from windows, furniture, stairs and playground equipment.

For this reason, avoid putting any furniture under windows, where it will tempt little climbers, and make sure there are catches or locks on all frames. This will go a long way to giving you peace of mind, but do make sure that all windows can be opened quickly by you, in case of a fire. Keep keys nearby but out of your child's reach – you could even tape them to the upper frame.

The majority of falls from windows happen during spring and summer, because they are more likely to be left open. If you need to open your windows, do so from the top rather than the bottom. If this is not possible, install safety bars or screens on the lower halves of windows that only an adult or older child can push out from the inside in an emergency.

Be sure to tie up all curtain and blind cords around wall brackets to keep them out of reach; cords with loops should be cut to prevent your child from strangling himself.

Staying safe on the stairs

Around 60,000 children under the age of five are injured falling down stairs every year.

● As soon as your child is able to climb up and down stairs, spend time with him teaching him how to do so safely. Young children (under the age of two and a half) might find it easier to crawl up stairs

Questions & Answers

How can I reduce the risk of my child getting an electric shock?
The most effective step you can take is to install plastic socket covers on all sockets that are not being used. It's also a good idea to get into the habit of unplugging appliances when not in use, and using socket covers.

Children may be tempted to chew on power cables, as well as tug them, and this can also be a cause of electrocution. Use cord shorteners to tidy up loose wires, and make sure cable is always held in place behind heavy furniture. Alternatively, staple or tape it to the floor or walls.

Check electric cable frequently and replace any worn cable. Never run cables or flexes under carpets or rugs.

rather than walk, and climb down stairs backwards, as if coming down a ladder.

● Never let your child climb up or down stairs unsupervised until you are absolutely sure of his competence.

● Make sure your banisters are sturdy, with less than 10cm (4in) between the posts. If the gaps are any larger than that, your baby or child could get his neck or head caught. Banisters with large gaps between them may need boarding up.

● Banisters should have no horizontal bars or slats – your child

THE BATHROOM CABINET
Your bathroom cabinet or first aid cupboard should be positioned well out of reach of your child. Medicines and other dangerous items should be kept locked away.

may use them as a ladder. If need be, remove them or board them up.

• Keep stairs clutter-free. If you are in the habit of leaving things on the stairs ready to take on the next trip, place a sturdy box in the hallway instead to accommodate these items.

• Leave a night light on in the hallway for older children needing to get up in the night.

Bathroom safety

The simplest way to avoid bathroom injuries is to make this room inaccessible unless your child is with an adult. This may mean installing a latch or lock on the outside of the door at adult height.

A child can drown in as little as 5cm (2in) of water, so it is not only the bath that poses a threat: toilet bowls, nappy buckets and sinks, for example, can be just as dangerous. There are other potential hazards to try to avoid as well.

• Keep toothpaste, mouthwashes, soaps and shampoos high up or in a cabinet with a safety latch or locks. Sharp objects, such as razor blades, scissors and nail clippers, should also be locked away.

NON-SLIP BATH
A non-slip bath mat or adhesive strips will protect your child from nasty bumps when he's in the bath.

Water temperature

Injuries caused by scalding bath water often involve large parts of the body. This is why it is important that you run the cold water into the bath before adding the hot water, and always test the temperature before letting your child get in. A child exposed to a very hot tap could sustain a third-degree burn, which requires hospitalization and skin grafts.

One of the most effective ways to prevent burns and scalds is to turn your hot-water thermostat down. Safety experts recommend that hot water should come out of your taps at no more than 45°C (113°F).

- Remove all electrical items, such as hairdryers, razors and radios, from the bathroom.
- Never throw used razor blades, toothbrushes or other potentially dangerous materials into the bathroom wastebasket.
- Check that shower doors or other surfaces are made of safety glass or shatterproof material.
- Throw away soap when it is small enough to fit inside your child's mouth. Children can choke on soap.
- Many accidents occur while a carer leaves a baby or toddler unattended "just for a minute" to answer the telephone. Take your child with you, invest in a cordless telephone or switch on the answering machine.

In the bath

Never, *under any circumstances*, leave your baby or child unsupervised in the bath. Children can drown in seconds. If you have to go to the door or phone, take your child out of the bath, wrap him in a towel and take him with you when you go to answer it. Or, ignore it!

Remember that bath seats and rings designed for young babies are meant to be bathing aids, not safety aids. They will not stop your child drowning if he is left unattended.

There are other important bathtime safety considerations.
- Place a non-slip mat or strips on the bottom of your bath.
- Always run the cold water before the hot, and then mix the water so

that it feels just warm. Test it with your inner wrist or elbow before putting your baby in the water.
- Always use both hands to lift your baby into and out of the bath.
- Cover taps with soft flannels during bathtime.

Toilets

- Get into the habit of keeping the toilet lid down at all times – fix on a toilet lock if you want to be particularly careful.
- Never leave toilet cleaner in the toilet bowl to soak. Wash it and flush it away.

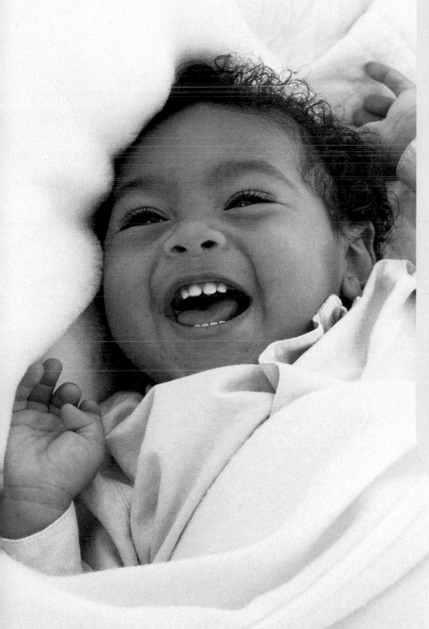

9-12
months

" In the space of **just a year** he really has developed into his own little person. "

DEE, mother of 12-month-old Cameron

" Feeding Nicole is **much simpler** now. I take some potatoes, vegetables and meat out of our main meal and mash it up for her. It's **better than ready-made** any day. "

CAROLINE, mother of Nicole, nine months

Feeding your older baby

Your baby's personality is starting to shine through, and as her sense of self grows, so does her desire for independence. Over the next few months she'll work hard at learning how to feed herself, and with your patience and praise she'll soon master this essential skill. Meanwhile, you can enjoy her company at the table – this is a great time to start letting her join in with family meals.

Advancing skills

Your baby now has regular mealtimes with three meals – breakfast, lunch and dinner – every day and two or three snacks as well. She can cope well with mashed or chopped food and uses finger foods to practise her chewing skills. There is now little she can't eat, so family meals can be easily adapted to feed your baby too. Carry on talking to her about what you are doing when you are preparing the meals and give her lots of praise.

Your baby's new skills make mealtimes easier:
- she can now chew; cope with different textures; and pick up shapes – talk to your health visitor if she is having difficulties with any of these
- her hand-eye coordination is developing fast, and learning how to feed herself is a natural step towards independence

- she's starting to recognize lots of familiar words such as "beaker" and "lunchtime"
- she loves interacting with people and will enjoy social get togethers such as mealtimes.

Introducing new tastes

Your older baby is becoming much more active – learning to crawl and then walk – which means she needs extra calories for energy and growth. She also needs a wide variety of nutrients in her diet, so now is a good time to introduce her to a broader range of foods. As her natural inclination is to explore everything she can get her hands on – including food – this is a great age to offer your baby new tastes, although as she enjoys some independence, she is also beginning to show clear food preferences.

Extra equipment

You will find the following useful as your baby becomes more experienced at feeding herself:

- **plastic feeding bowl** with a suction pad to prevent her flinging food all over the floor

- **plastic bib** with a moulded tray to catch the food that doesn't make it into her mouth

- **portable highchair** that screws or clips onto a table top – a great help when you are out visiting friends or relatives or on holiday.

Encouraging self-feeding

Your baby is developing a strong sense of herself in the family and of her daily routines. She'll start to look forward to mealtimes, and will recognize the cues that mean food is on the way. She'll also want to be just like you – which means feeding herself, rather than being fed by you. Encouraging your baby to self-feed means that, for a while at least, mealtimes will take longer and be messier. To begin with, your baby will probably keep turning over the spoon before it reaches her mouth. But as her finger and hand skills develop, she'll soon master the art of feeding herself.

Help her reach this milestone by:
• giving her lots of chances to practise – and ignoring the mess!
• making sure she's getting enough food in her mouth by helping her load her spoon and slipping in mouthfuls with your own spoon in between attempts
• serving her food that will stay on the spoon more easily – mashed potato with cheese, thick yogurts and fromage frais, for example
• resisting the temptation to take over – letting her have a go, and eventually succeed, will do wonders for her confidence.

Talk to your health visitor if your child shows no interest in self-feeding.

Getting the portions right

Every baby's appetite is different – and can change from day to day. This means it can be hard to judge how much food your baby needs. Remember that a baby's stomach can't hold very much and therefore she'll need to eat more frequently than you.

It's good to encourage your baby to feed at regular times but accept also that your baby will probably need a snack in between mealtimes to help fill the gaps. When she's uninterested, let her out of her highchair after 10 minutes or so and offer her another meal or snack a couple of hours later.

Teething and eating

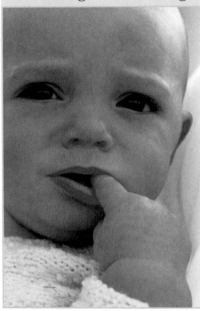

When your baby is teething don't be surprised if she goes off her food. Over the next couple of months she'll have lots of teeth coming through and, although some babies take teething in their stride and show no ill-effects, others become fretful and irritable.

The common signs of teething include swollen, reddened gums, excessive drooling, an inflamed cheek, mild cough and even a low-grade fever. Your baby will also want to bite down on anything she can get in her mouth.

If pain and discomfort affect your baby's appetite, she'll need more milk for a while. She may also refuse to drink from a beaker, despite having previously loved the independence it gave her. Bottle-feeding your baby again shouldn't be a problem as long as it's only short term.

Meanwhile, chewing and sucking on firm-textured finger food that becomes soft for easy swallowing can help soothe your baby's gums – and offer her some extra nutrition at the same time. You could also try, for example, a frozen banana or chilled wholemeal crust. But never leave her alone with food in case she chokes. Commercially made teething biscuits are best avoided as they contain a lot of sugar. Cold food – such as chilled puréed apple – may also be more appealing than warm food.

INDEPENDENT FEEDING
The time will come when your baby wants her independence. Allowing her to feed herself will boost her confidence, and she will quickly master the skills she needs.

Don't allow your child to carry a bottle or food around between meals or snacks as this will lessen her appetite, and a family rule of no food between meals will increase the likelihood of her eating more at mealtimes.

Planning her meals

Your baby should have at least one daily portion of fish, meat, egg, lentils or beans (these are the best sources of protein and iron) as well as food from the four main food groups every day. These groups are:

● dairy products such as cheese, yogurt or full-fat fromage frais (don't rely on just cheese for protein – use meat, fish or egg yolks, too)

● starchy foods such as potatoes, bread, noodles, rice, pasta, couscous and breakfast cereals

● fruit and vegetables: offer a selection of fresh fruit and vegetables so she gets used to different tastes and textures

Expert tip

Your baby can now eat the same food as you as long as it doesn't contain added salt, sugar or honey. You should also avoid giving her:

● foods that carry a high risk of food poisoning (such as mould-ripened cheese, liver pâté and soft-boiled eggs)

● whole nuts (ground nuts are fine, unless there is a history of allergies, in which case you should avoid all nuts).

When can my baby join in family meals?

Now is a great time for your baby to join in with family meals. She's a little individual with a real personality and she enjoys having fun with everyone. Her ability to understand language is coming on fast and she's really trying to communicate with you. Even if she doesn't have the same food, feeding your baby when the rest of the family is eating together has lots of benefits.

A FAMILY AFFAIR
Children who regularly eat meals with the family are less likely to be fussy eaters and more likely to try a wider range of foods.

It's good to eat together

Family mealtimes are about more than just making sure everyone is getting fed – they are also social occasions and great opportunities for your baby to learn about good table manners and conversation.

Eating with your baby will also make her more adventurous when it comes to food. A baby who won't eat green beans may change her mind when she sees everyone else enjoying them.

Keep the atmosphere light and easy-going by:
★ planning family meals around your baby – if she's tired, eating together won't be fun for you or her
★ not expecting too much – if your baby turns her nose up at the food on her plate, don't take it personally, there could be various explanations for why she's not hungry today
★ ignoring the mess – have lots of paper towels handy for cleaning up as she goes.

- meat and fish, such as soft, flaked white fish, well-chopped chicken or lamb, and meat alternatives such as a few well-cooked lentils or beans.

   Babies' appetites are very changeable, however, so check your child's diet over a week rather than a day. Talk to your health visitor if you think she isn't eating all the foods she needs for good nutrition.

Meal ideas

- Breakfast

Yogurt smoothie and toast; porridge with dried fruit; Weetabix and milk with grated pear.

- Lunch/dinner

Lasagne; sausages with mashed potato and vegetables; cut-up jacket potato with hummus/avocado/baked beans.

- Puddings

Baked bananas and full-fat plain yogurt; bread and butter pudding; wholemeal pancakes with fresh fruit; canned fruit in natural juice.

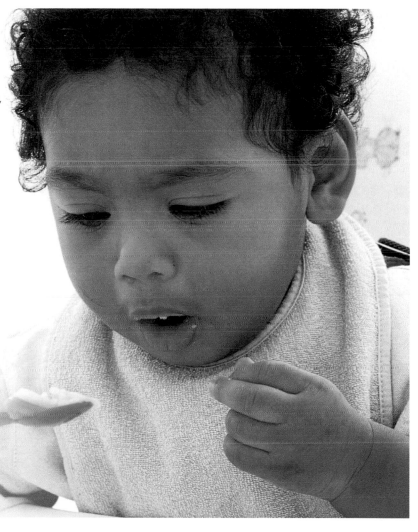

Questions & Answers

My baby is now nine months old and she still has no teeth. Should I be worried about this?

Many babies at nine months are still toothless – and some even make it to their first year without a single tooth in sight. Late teething needn't affect your baby's move onto chunkier food. Babies with and without teeth use their gums for chewing until their molars appear in the middle of the second year.

My baby doesn't seem to eat very much. Should I be encouraging her to eat more?

Your baby's tummy will fill up quickly on solid food so when she's had enough, don't insist she has one last mouthful. This may put her off the food she's eating as well as making her feel upset and resentful. Talk to your health visitor if your baby:

- tries to store food in her cheeks rather than swallow
- refuses to accept textured food.

Tips for healthy eating

One of the best ways you can help your baby to grow up fit and healthy is to help her develop healthy eating habits now. These guidelines will help.

● **If she rejects something today, try again a few days later.**
Babies' tastes are notoriously fickle and just because she appears not to like something now there's no reason to assume she won't enjoy it another time. It can take 10–20 times of offering for a baby to accept a new food, and sometimes even longer.

● **Praise her when she eats well.**
Your baby will quickly realize that healthy, natural food is good for her if you tell her how clever she is when she eats it.

● **Avoid "sugary" treats.**
Sugar and sugary foods contain what is termed "empty calories" – lots of sugar and energy but little else of nutritional value.

● **Offer healthy snacks.**
It may be easier to reach for the biscuit tin when your baby is hungry between meals, but it's worth getting her used to nutritious snacks.

● **Don't allow your child to graze between meals.**
If your child sits in her highchair for a meal or snack every two to three hours she will not be hungry in between – don't allow her to carry food or drink around with her.

Milk needs

Your baby should still be having at least 500–600ml (17–20fl oz) of breast milk or formula a day (this is equivalent to about two breastfeeds). Around this age, however, she may start to wean herself off the breast.

Losing interest in sucking can happen if your baby is eating lots of solids and is good at using a beaker. It may, however, only be temporary. Perhaps your baby is teething, in which case sucking can put pressure on painful gums. Your baby is also curious about the world around her – and she may be easily distracted if people are in the room or the television is on. Feed her in a quiet room without distractions.

Meanwhile, check that your baby is getting her full milk quota by offering her formula in her beaker. If she doesn't like this, supplement her diet with plenty of full-fat yogurts and hard cheese.

● **Avoid fast food.**
Pizzas, chicken nuggets and chips are all high in fats and salt and may contain additives too. If your child eats these foods regularly she may have a greater risk of developing health problems as an adult.

Thirst quenchers

Your baby may still be resisting using a beaker, but it's worth persisting. Drinking from a beaker is better for speech development and for her teeth.

Give your baby water between meals if she seems thirsty. During the summer when she is losing fluid through sweat, you should also offer her a drink of water a couple of times during the day. Don't make a habit of giving her juice too often – maximum of 120ml (4fl oz) a day –

she'll love the sweeter taste and quickly refuse anything else. Too much fruit juice can cause diarrhoea, nappy rash and contribute to poor dental health.

Watch out, food about!

Your baby is now much more skilled with her hands. She has mastered the pincer grasp and can pick up anything she comes across using her thumb and forefinger. This means she can guide pieces of food into her mouth more accurately – so self-feeding is getting much less messy.

She's also figured out how to "let go" of things. Be prepared for lots of dropping and picking up games (she drops, you pick up). By the end of her first year, she'll have discovered how to throw as well.

" I always make extra for Rashmi and then freeze it for meals the following week. This saves me time – and also makes me feel less frustrated if she doesn't eat much. "

NAWSHEEN is mum to Rashmi, 11 months

" I breastfed Sam for **two years** and it was a special time. When he finally stopped, I felt a little sad, but mostly I was pleased that we'd done it. I'll always know I gave him the **best start**. "

EMMA, mother of two-and-a-half-year-old Sam

How long should I breastfeed for?

How long you continue to breastfeed for is up to you – and your baby, of course. Many babies who are exclusively breastfed, and start taking cows' milk only after their first birthday, tend to want to go on nursing for a long time. Others, though, phase out breastfeeding gradually towards the end of their first year.

Changing preferences

If you have chosen to mix breast and bottle you may find your baby starts to prefer her bottle as she nears the end of her first year. This is because the milk from a bottle flows more easily and quickly than the milk from a breast, and older babies tend to become more impatient if they know there's a faster option! By this stage you'll know that your baby has had huge benefits by being breastfed.

Dropping feeds

You'll probably find you drop feeds quite naturally during the second half of the first year. As your baby gets a taste for solid food, and enjoys the experience of sitting in her highchair and participating in family meals, she'll often prefer that to being nursed on your lap.

Some mothers feel that by this stage they're ready to stop breastfeeding. If you are in this position and don't feel your baby is feeding any less, or isn't cutting down her feeds as quickly as you'd like, try this step-by-step plan to faster weaning.

Step 1: Skip the lunchtime breastfeed and offer a drink from a cup instead.

Step 2: After a few days, skip the mid-morning feed and offer a drink of water instead.

Step 3: Skip the final evening feed or cut out the morning feed. You will then be left with occasional snacks, if your baby still has these, and one sizeable feed night or morning.

Step 4: Cut out the occasional feeds by distracting your baby at times when she wants to come onto your lap for a feed. Another person – ideally your partner – can help by

playing with her when she really wants a breastfeed.

Step 5: Cut out the final morning or evening breastfeed by changing your routine at that time of the day. Again, a partner or another family member can help by being around

Myths about giving up

When you give up is your decision. In particular, you don't have to give up when:

- your baby cuts her first tooth
- she bites you (just say "no" very firmly and move her away from the breast – she'll soon realize that biting means no access to your milk, and won't continue to bite)
- she starts on solid food
- she starts to feed herself.

DISTRACTION TECHNIQUES
Reading a book with your babies allows them to feel close to you while also taking their minds off wanting a breastfeed.

Expert tip

A final breastfeed can be a difficult moment for you. Far better, therefore, not to have a formal "final feed". Simply cut down and down until your baby or toddler is hardly ever feeding at the breast. Then, when she does want the breast just try to distract her, but don't refuse completely if you can see it means a lot to her. That way you'll probably find your final breastfeed goes unmarked, because you'll never know she won't come back for "one more bit" one day.

to distract. If your baby has a security blanket or special cuddly toy, this can be very useful here as well. Try to introduce some new "treat" into the picture - maybe a cup of warm milk for bedtime, or a musical tape, or if it's the morning feed make a big treat out of dad taking your baby downstairs for an early play.

Giving up breastfeeding

Ending breastfeeding is much easier for both you and your baby if you do it gradually. Give up quickly, and you're far more likely to suffer

engorged breasts as your body hasn't been able to react fast enough to the fact that you've cut down on so many feeds. Take it slowly, and your body adjusts with you.

Weaning slowly is also far more pleasant for your baby, who may hardly notice her breastfeeds are becoming less frequent. If you wean her too quickly she's likely to be confused and hurt by your rejection of her needs: your breasts have represented her strongest security to date. Abruptly withdrawing them from her may make her anxious.

Breastfeeding an older baby or toddler

Toddlers don't "need" breast milk for health reasons in the way that younger babies do. However, there's still evidence that the immunological advantages of breast milk continue to be useful. Breastfeeding can also:

● comfort your child when she has a fall or hurts herself

● offer an occasional "safe haven" at a time when she's branching out and sometimes finds the world a bit overwhelming

● continue to reinforce the special relationship she has with her mum.

If you and your toddler are happy to go on breastfeeding, that's fine. In many parts of the world children are routinely breastfed until at least the age of three, and sometimes even until they begin school at five.

Do what's right for you

In the West, however, weaning has been speeded up and it's uncommon to see babies of more than six months being breastfed. This adds to a general sense that once a baby is in the second half of her first year she should have given up – by contrast, though, it's very common to see older babies out and about with bottles.

You shouldn't have to put up with negativity and criticism if you choose to breastfeed your older baby, but some mothers say they do get a lot of unkind comments. In Norway, a country with far better breastfeeding rates than either the UK or the US, breastfeeding toddlers are a common sight.

Staying close to your child

You'll want to find new ways of being close to your child now you're not breastfeeding. There may be some special time of the day when you can cuddle up together – sharing a book can replace the intimacy of your nursing together. Remember that you won't "lose" the closeness you've built up through breastfeeding: on the contrary, you'll go on building on it throughout the rest of your life.

How will you feel when you stop?

Some women say they're relieved when they decide to stop breastfeeding – they felt it had become tying and they like the sense of freedom and of having their bodies back to themselves. It's good to move on and to feel your child is getting older, but for many mums there's also a tinge of regret that this phase is over.

If you hope to have more children, you may like to look forward to breastfeeding again with a new baby in the years ahead. If this is likely to be your only or your final child, though, you may feel a sense of sadness that a chapter of your life is now closing, particularly if you have fed several children.

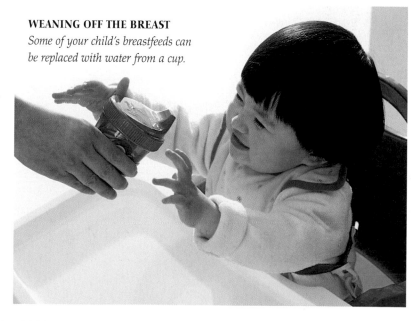

WEANING OFF THE BREAST
Some of your child's breastfeeds can be replaced with water from a cup.

" Hannah started using her first words – she called our dog 'woof' – just before her **first birthday,** but I had a strong sense that she had been building up to those **words for months.** "

JACK is dad to 18-month-old Hannah

Learning to talk

From the moment your baby is born, and often before, you will notice his reactions to voices and other sounds. By the end of his first year he will have become a collector of all the information he needs to produce his first words. The quest begins as soon as he is born because learning about the joys of human interaction has its roots in the first few weeks of life when you and your baby start to get to know one another.

The drive to communicate

From when he was a newborn baby, your child has been an active communicator. At first, his cries and burps relate only to how he is feeling, whether he is hungry, tired, needs a fresh nappy or has too much wind. Although he doesn't yet know that he is sending out a message, your response teaches him that his cries have consequences – they bring rewards. It's not long before he begins to use crying to express specific needs and focus it on the people who are likely to do something about them. He is already beginning to communicate.

Your first conversations are all about kindness, reassurance and making him feel safe. Most parents chatter away to their babies without really being aware of it: "Hello baby, have you woken up for your feed?"

"Over to Daddy, now – he wants to change your nappy." "Ooh, you don't like me taking off your vest, do you?" To your baby this is nothing more than a meaningless string of sounds, but they make him feel calm and attended to nonetheless.

Using all his senses

Your baby's rapid development in his first year involves all his senses – vision, hearing, touch, taste and smell. As soon as he is born, they help him to know who and what is important to him, and gradually over the coming months he learns to use his senses to gather information. Even if he can hear, he must learn to listen. As soon as he can focus, he needs to learn to direct his attention so he can begin to recognize gestures, facial expressions, familiar objects and movements.

Checklist

Babies pass these talking milestones in their first year:

- cooing after six weeks
- babbling from six months; increasing experimentation with sounds
- begin to use specific sounds in specific contexts, for example "woof" for all animals
- by nine months, understand "no" and "bye"
- by age one, recognize some words and respond to requests such as "clap your hands"; may speak one or two words.

The basics of talk

Most of the time we communicate so effortlessly, we fail to appreciate how complex human communication is. However, to understand how children learn to talk, it helps to separate out some of its different elements: these are communication, language and speech.

Beginning to communicate

It seems that children are born not just to speak but also to interact with other people – their parents in the first instance, but soon everyone else around them. Long before your baby uses words, she uses cries and gestures to make her meaning clear and responds to and learns to read the gestures and facial expressions of those who care for her.

At first, your interaction with your baby is made up of stroking, rocking, smiling and eye contact – gestures that convey your feelings more effectively than words can. They tell your baby that you love her and are interested in her. She understands emotion long before she can talk.

GESTURES
Smiles, touch and eye contact tell your baby you are interested in who she is.

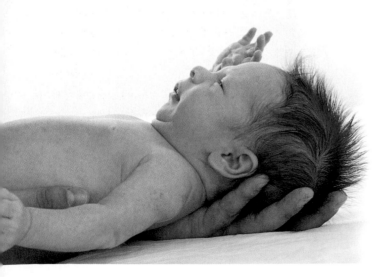

Gestures, facial expression and body language are a major part of communication in these early months and continue to be so throughout life. Think how much you use them to enhance your speech and interpret what you hear. They are an essential fall-back when a meaning is unclear or a language is foreign to you.

However, human communication is also about referring to and describing the world, and this is the next step your child takes towards becoming a talker. Once she has established what words do and how they relate to things, it is only a matter of time before she is naming what she sees – "woof", "bus", "drink" and "mum".

What is language?

Language in general, and grammar in particular, is what distinguishes humans from other animals. This system we have of combining words into meaningful sequences enables us to give shape to our ideas and thoughts and convey them to others.

One of the really distinctive features of our capacity to learn language is our ability to be creative with sentences. Although we use some expressions over and over again, we are constantly producing new sentences that we have never said before and that we have never heard anyone else say either.

FIRST WORDS
Once your child has learned the trick of linking the sounds he hears to things that are important to him, he can attempt any number of words.

Checklist

Language is made up of:

- phonemes such as /b/ and /p/ – the smallest sound units of language. They are speech sounds, not letters, and there are about 40 in English

- morphemes – the smallest meaningful units of language. "Do" is a morpheme, but so is "un" because it changes or adds meaning

- syntax – the combination of words into phrases and sentences.

By two and a half, most children are using the three main components of a complex language system. They learn the rules of *phonology* as they combine sounds into words. Then they get to grips with *syntax* as they combine words in the correct order to make up phrases and sentences such as "Get ball" or "Pasta all gone". Although these are simple requests and observations, they are *semantic* (they have a precise meaning). In fact, children start to put words together as soon as they want to communicate more complicated meanings.

Children's language skills are not simply confined to what they are able to say – they also need to understand what they hear. An essential part of learning to talk is using what they know about language to work out what others are saying.

Can other creatures talk?

Do any animals other than humans have language? Observers of animal communication have made some fascinating discoveries.

- The North American cicada has four different calls, each one with a different message. The vervet monkey has 36 calls.

- Bees dance in a pattern to direct other bees to nearby pollen supplies.

- Dolphins can communicate specific information to other dolphins.

- Mynah birds and parrots mimic speech, but there is no evidence that they can understand any of it.

- Chimpanzees and gorillas are the only animals with anything that resembles a human capacity for communication. They do not have the vocal apparatus to speak, but they can be taught to communicate using sign language, keyboards and cards. In teaching programmes, some have learned to use hundreds of signs and understand even more.

However, even the cleverest gorillas and chimpanzees are able to form only the most basic sentences. They do not come close to being as creative with language as the average two-year-old human being.

Finding her voice

Your baby's first sounds tend to be nasal because her voice box (larynx) is high up, close to her mouth, and her throat (pharynx) is short. She becomes able to make speech sounds as her larynx descends and her pharynx lengthens. This is happening rapidly by the end of her first year and is complete by age three.

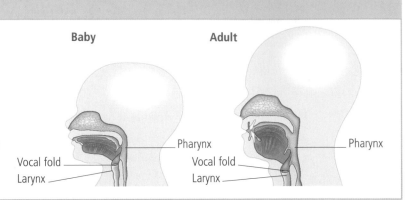

Baby   Adult

Pharynx

Pharynx

Vocal fold

Larynx

Vocal fold

Larynx

Practising her speech

Your baby's speech is made up of phonemes – all the sounds of the language or languages that she is learning in her first year, usually from her mum and dad. The earliest sounds she makes are not specific to any language but, by 12 months or so, she is already specializing in the ones she will need to use.

Making speech sounds is not an easy task for a baby and relies as much on her physical development as her growing ability to think. She has to be able to control her head, bring her lips together deliberately, move her tongue up and down and use the soft palate at the top of her mouth to produce them. All of this has to be coordinated with her breathing and the movement of her voice box (larynx). To begin with, your baby will have little control over this, but by her first birthday she will be producing a range of

SOUND PLAY
She loves to practise sounds, and uses them with all the variety and expression of real speech as she chats to her toys and "reads" from her books.

sounds that are more and more like real speech. Soon she will be producing her first attempts at words.

Critical time?

Do children have to learn language at a particular stage in their life, and is the chance lost for ever if they are not given enough stimulation?

No scientist would prevent a child from learning language, so answers to these questions have to be based on rare examples of children who have been raised in isolation with no meaningful contact with humans. From these studies it appears that a child who is not exposed to language in the first eight or nine years is very unlikely to learn language.

Although language learning is innate, it appears to rely on experiences during key periods for its development. The first six months of life seem to be critical for homing

"It's incredible how rapidly Sam's speech has developed since those early babbles during his first year. His speech seems so confident now."

TESS is mum to three-year-old Sam

in on the sounds of the child's native language, and in the years between one and five, grammar is more easily acquired than at any other time in life. There is evidence, too, that a child's early talking skills continue to have a bearing on the way the brain is configured once it becomes more specialized in language during adolescence.

What is certain is that the first three years of life are a critically important learning period for children. After the first year, language is the key that helps children unlock many of their discoveries about the world, enables them to order and express their thoughts and ideas, and opens the door to literacy.

Talking milestones

Babies acquire speech skills in the same order, whatever their language. These are the stages your baby passes through en route to becoming a talker.

● She makes non-verbal sounds and uses intonation to express what she wants. She points to ask for things or makes a noise to get attention.

● She uses her own versions of words that are understood within the family, for example, "bi-bi" becomes the family word for biscuit. The rise and fall of her voice is still very important in letting you know what she means.

● She begins to use and speak her first conventional words.

● She uses single words to mean more than the thing she is referring to. For example "drink" begins to mean "Can you get me a drink?"

● She uses two words together: "Mummy gone" or "More ball". Although she knows what she means, some phrases are not obvious to unfamiliar listeners and need to be deciphered by trial and error.

● She combines two or three words to make sentences that include an object or person (a noun) and something happening (a verb) – "Dog eat dinner".

● She links ideas using conjunctions such as "and" and uses word endings such as "ed" to make different tenses.

How should I talk to my baby?

Babies become better talkers if they are spoken to a great deal by their parents and carers, but it's not simply a matter of the amount of speech they hear. There is a characteristic way in which most people talk to babies that helps them to focus on and absorb the sounds and words of a language. Experts call it "parentese" or "caregiver talk".

What is parentese?

Do parents need to be instructed in parentese? Most likely not at all. Just as your baby came into the world wired and ready to learn a language, your response to him seems to be programmed, too. You instinctively adjust your tone and style of language to suit his needs. Most grandparents do it quite naturally, too, and even young children seem to know that they have to change their speech when they are addressing babies and younger children. Here are the key features:

★ You speak in a higher-pitched voice and more slowly than normal, with clear pauses at the end of your sentences.

TIME FOR A TALK
The best time for a talk is when your baby is wide awake but not hungry and looks ready to play.

A FRIENDLY GREETING
Move in close when you start the conversation so he can focus on your face and meet your gaze. Start off the conversation with a broad smile and a question – "Hello my beautiful Toby, are you all nice and clean now that you've had your bath?"

PAUSE AND WAIT
Now pause and wait. He may just look straight into your face with a big smile at first because it takes him a little while to work up his own response – perhaps a noise, a body movement or a wave of the hands. If he is beginning to coo or babble, he may offer a string of sounds.

TIMING YOUR REPLY
Either copy his sounds or comment on them, "Oh, that was a good whoop." Don't leave it too long before you reply – he may lose the connection between what you say and what he did, and the dialogue will be broken. Keep the conversation going until his interest begins to wane and he looks away.

★ You exaggerate your intonation, adopting a sing-song voice that emphasizes important words.

★ Your sentences are short, simple and grammatical and also tend to be very repetitive.

★ You repeat back what your child has said or "recast" it to make it a little more complicated. Your baby says "shoe" and you respond with "Yes, you're putting on your shoe – it's a blue shoe".

★ Your vocabulary is "concrete" in that it tends to refer to people or things that are present rather than ideas and things that cannot be seen.

The dance of interaction

First dialogues with your baby may only last a few minutes, but they contain some essential ingredients of conversation – good listening and turn taking. So the next time you ask your baby a question that you assume will be rhetorical, wait for a moment and see if he has something to tell you in return (between two and seven seconds is the ideal pause). Not everyone gets the timing right at first, and babies are often thwarted in their first attempts at conversation. They get an enthusiastic welcome from a visitor, who then looks away to talk to someone else at the critical moment when they are just working up to waving their arms or offering an expressive grunt by way of a reply.

Babies love rituals that follow a set pattern and allow them to take control. When a conversation is working well it is like a dance of interaction in which both partners know exactly what to expect.

Setting up little dialogues like this is a great way to let your baby know that he is being listened to and is important. He is being acknowledged as a conversational partner and learning that it is worthwhile trying to communicate.

Your baby's name

The very first word that is likely to have meaning for your baby is his own name. He hears it whenever a familiar or new face says "hello" or "goodbye", and it occurs continually in the speech he hears from his parents and carers. Usually by the time he is four or five months old, he understands that his name has a special relevance to him, although it will be some time before he is able to say it himself.

Fine-tuning the sounds

Towards the end of his first year, your baby has a whole battery of sounds at his disposal, spoken with all the conviction and variety of real speech. He no longer tolerates being left out of conversations and can now shout to get attention when he is ignored. Babies of this age really like to make their presence felt, especially when everyone else is silent. Solemn occasions in churches are a favourite time to exercise his voice – the echo is very rewarding.

LOOK, JAMES!
Now he recognizes his own name, it is easier to initiate games and chats and direct his attention to interesting sights and activities.

Your response to this sociable little person is changing too. Now it seems positively rude not to address someone who is so obviously ready for conversational give and take.

- Make time to talk directly to your baby, particularly if life is becoming more hectic now that you are back at work. He needs face-to-face talk with lots of emphasis on key labelling words – "your cup", "Daddy's shoes" – rather than a sea of chatter.
- Even if you are not much given to emotional displays, emphasize your gestures and emotions when you talk to him – they give him vital clues to what you are saying.
- Try to understand his gestures and sounds. Follow his gaze and hazard a guess at what he might be labelling as a "bon". He will be thrilled if you hit on the correct thing. Repeat it back to him – "balloon" – and add some detail, but don't expect him to copy the word correctly.

Working up to words

Imagine your nine-month-old hears the following: "nowletsseewhatyouve gotuptoohdearyouvegotawetnappy poorbabynowonderyouvebeencrying wedbetterchangeyou". To understand this stream of sounds, he has to listen carefully and learn to recognize where one word ends and another begins. "Now let's see what you've got up to.

HIDE AND SEEK
Unveiling a hidden toy never fails to surprise, but don't make the game too difficult or add too many variations.

Expert tips

The best games for babies over six months are repetitive and predictable. It helps them to feel in control of events.

● Put a light scarf over your head and ask your baby to "find Mummy". Stay close so he can pull it off and reveal your face. Now drape it lightly over his head and ask "Where's Joey?". He will soon learn to pull it off himself.

● When your baby is nine or ten months old cover up a toy within his reach, letting him watch you as you do it. Now ask him to find the toy. Look surprised and delighted and praise him when he does.

● Hold him facing a mirror and point out what you both can see. "These are Joey's eyes." "This is Joey's nose." "This is Mummy's nose." Soon he will be pointing to his own nose on request, or finding the dolly's eyes or the teddy's ears.

Oh dear, you've got a wet nappy. Poor baby, no wonder you've been crying. We'd better change you."

How do babies manage to do that? The answer is that, at first, he may not really break up the speech stream at all. It may just be a wash of interesting and engaging sounds that leave him feeling reassured and attended to. But as his listening skills improve, he begins to extract some important parts from the sounds he is hearing and decode them by comparing them with the dictionary of words he is forming in his head. You give him clues by slowing your speech, exaggerating the boundaries between words and speaking with expression and shifts of intonation.

Baby body language

Babies start to decipher what people around them mean by watching and listening, and what they understand is made up of all sorts of bits of information – what was said, who said it, when it was said and where it was said. They learn that outstretched arms mean "Come here" long before they understand the words that go with the gesture. Although at first it may be difficult to know whether your baby has really understood the message, it's not long before he is using these familiar gestures himself at the

GETTING THE POINT
Now that he can point he can direct your attention to what he desires most.

appropriate times. He knows that putting his arms out and smiling to you has a specific effect – he will be picked up and cuddled. Yet when a comparative stranger asks for a hug from your 10-month-old baby, he may shake his head vigorously – a gesture that is every bit as effective as verbal language.

Over the previous months, your baby has developed hand-eye coordination and can pick up and examine interesting objects within his reach. By nine months, your baby can follow your finger and look wherever you point. Now you have a useful tool for focusing his

attention on interesting events and sights and the fascinating details in his picture books.

Roots of language

Your baby can direct your attention, too. To begin with, he will simply point – "I want it". However, by about 10 months he will point at an object and then to you, and use his own sound for what he wants. The message here is different because it clearly shows he is aware that you know the word that he is using – "I know that you know what I mean". Here we have the roots of spoken language – "reference". Your baby is referring to the world around him. Without this simple shared reference it would be almost impossible for him to learn language at all.

Gradually, babies begin to expect certain words in certain contexts and fix in mind what they mean. By eight months your baby may follow simple instructions, especially if there is a visual cue such as "say bye-bye to Mummy" (plus wave), or "give it to Daddy" (plus an outstretched hand). He soon starts to show that he knows even more words, looking for the cat when it is mentioned in passing or picking up his cup when someone asks for a drink.

A social being

Towards the end of your baby's first year, you are left in no doubt that he is fully equipped with almost everything he needs for effective communication.

• He can gesture welcome and rejection, imitate a full range of facial expressions, shout deep disapproval, and then change his tone to convey unrestrained joy.

• He enjoys dancing and romping, clapping games, music and songs, and can produce a few magical little scales and tunes of his own.

• He will imitate some words if he can manage the right sounds but may still have no idea what they mean –

something an older sibling may take advantage of from time to time.

• He may also have one or two odd little words of his own, but often they can only be interpreted by people who know him very well.

In his first year your baby has developed irresistible social skills alongside his language skills, and the two are now becoming enmeshed. He is discovering that speech is a very effective way of being sociable.

READY TO PLAY
Your baby is a more interesting playmate now that he has some social skills.

Expert tips

Start sharing books when your baby is about six months old.

• Choose simple board books with realistic pictures – they are easier for him to recognize than cartoons.

• Don't be put off if he wants to chew the book rather than look at it.

• Point and chat about what you see, but stop as soon as he loses interest.

Talking with books

Books are a great way of interacting with your young child. Being read to helps to focus her attention precisely on words because she has pictures to refer to while she is hearing them. She will also love the attention, cuddles and close contact that goes hand in hand with sharing a book.

● Just a few favourite books are all you need at first because your child will enjoy repetition as much as novelty. She is proud of what she knows and wants to share it repeatedly. Choose books with realistic recognizable pictures that reflect your child's everyday experiences. She will enjoy joining in – lifting flaps to find hidden surprises and making animal noises in the right places.

● As a baby, your child may have simply pointed at the pictures, but now she is actively listening for words. Comment on what is happening on each page. Ask an occasional question – "What is the bear doing now?" – but not so many that it becomes a test; she will lose interest, especially if she is struggling to form words.

● By the age of two, children begin to enjoy books with a story and start to focus on sequences and cause and effect. Tell the story in your own words – it will bring it to life. The more children hear people modelling stories, the more they want to do it themselves.

Golden rules

Adults often feel that they have to be in control of children to show them what is what, but this can lead to very dull interaction, with one party calling the shots and the other reacting. Spend time following the communication lead of your child. Begin by simply watching what she is doing; then venture a comment on some aspect of it: "You're putting the elephant in the truck now." Try to expand on her reply to extend her vocabulary and understanding. "The elephant's very big isn't he… is he going to fit, do you think?" Don't try to distract your child away from the focus of her attention – go with it.

It's very easy for adults to anticipate their child's interests and needs and supply all the dialogue without her having to say much at all. She responds with a nod or shake of the head while you chatter on relentlessly. Make it a habit to listen carefully to her and be patient if you don't understand at first. Think of the effort she is putting into these first utterances and value them accordingly.

When she gets things wrong it's because she has limited words at her disposal and so is using what she has to elicit more information. Give her the correct word in a positive way rather than starting with a "no".

Avoiding baby talk

Perhaps one of the most important messages of this book is that you should be natural with your child. Although the parentese style of talk (see page 148) helps babies to focus on language, some parents feel they need to go further and use a special vocabulary, too. Dogs become "bow wows"; cats are "kitty-cats"; trains are "chuff-chuffs" and cars are "broom-brooms". Babytalk like this is of no particular value, and must at times be puzzling for a child, particularly if she spends time in settings where everyone uses the proper words.

The only really useful baby words are your child's own – her first attempts at words based on what she can manage to say. For a while a cushion may be a "pushun" because she can't quite produce a /k/ sound, or a fish, a "dit" until she can say /f/ and /sh/. However adorable you find these early versions of words, be happy to relinquish them as soon as she does. She shouldn't be made to feel that her baby pronunciation is so cute it is something that she needs to hold on to.

GOOD LISTENERS
Friends who listen with interest teach your child that her talk is important.

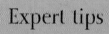

Expert tips

Try these 10 tips for keeping the conversation going.

- Actively engage in your child's earliest communication.
- Listen carefully and value what she has to say.
- Follow her communication lead.
- Expand on what she says.
- Show that you are interested in what she has to say and that it is important to you.
- Be natural – don't use "baby language" or try to "teach" her how to speak.
- Engage in her play.
- Tell stories that she can understand.
- Give her confidence to keep on communicating.
- Help her speak to other people by translating the words she says that are hard to understand.

Useful contacts

Association for Post-Natal Illness
145 Dawes Road,
London SW6 7EB
Tel: 020 7386 0868
www.apni.org

Association of Breastfeeding Mothers (ABM)
Helpline (24 hours): 020 7813 1481
www.abm.me.uk
Gives mother-to-mother breastfeeding support and up-to-date breastfeeding information.

Asthma UK
Providence House
Providence Place
London N1 0NT
Helpline: 0845 701 0203
www.asthma.org.uk

BabyCentre.com/safety/
Offers comprehensive online advice on baby and child safety.

BLISS
68 South Lambeth Road
London SW8 1RL
Helpline: 0500 618 140
www.bliss.org.uk
Offers help and support to families of premature and sick babies, funds research and campaigns for the improvement of neonatal service.

British Allergy Association
No. 3 White Oak Square
London Road
Swanley
Kent BR8 7AG
Helpline: 01322 619 864
www.allergyuk.org.uk

British Nutrition Foundation
High Holborn House
52-54 High Holborn
London WC1V 6RQ
Tel: 020 7404 6504
www.nutrition.org.uk

BSI (British Standards Institution)
389 Chiswick High Road
London W4 4AL
Tel: 020 8996 9000
www.bsi-global.com
Sets safety standards for British products, including toys and nursery equipment.

Caesarean Support Network
55 Cooli Drive
Douglas
Isle of Man 1M2 2HF
Tel: 01624 661 269 (after 6pm)
Advice on breastfeeding after a Caesarean section.

Child Accident Prevention Trust (CAPT)
18-20 Farringdon Lane
London EC1R 3HA
Tel: 020 7608 3828
www.capt.org.uk
Provides useful advice about all aspects of child safety.

Coeliac UK
PO Box 220
High Wycombe
Buckinghamshire HP11 2HY
Helpline: 0870 444 8804
www.coeliac.co.uk

Cry-sis
BM Cry-sis
London WC1N 3XX
Helpline: 020 7404 5011
www.cry-sis.org.uk
Provides emotional support and practical advice for parents dealing with a baby's crying and sleep problems.

Foundation for the Study of Infant Deaths (FSID)
Artillery House
11-19 Artillery Row
London SW1P 1RT
Helpline: 0870 787 0554
www.sids.org.uk/fsid/
Offers support and education to parents and professionals on reducing the risk of Sudden Infant Death Syndrome (SIDS).

Gingerbread
7 Sovereign Close
Sovereign Court
London E1W 3HW
Helpline: 0800 018 4318
Office: 020 7488 9300
www.gingerbread.org.uk
Practical support and help for lone-parent families.

La Leche League (GB)
PO Box 29
West Bridgford
Nottingham NG2 7NP
Helpline (24 hours): 0845 456 1886
www.laleche.org.uk
Offers help and information to mothers wishing to breastfeed.

MAMA
(Meet–A–Mum Association)
376 Bideford Green
Linslade
Leighton Buzzard LU7 2TY
Tel: 01525 217 064
www.mama.org.uk
Aims to help mothers who feel
depressed and isolated when their
babies are born, through local groups of
mothers sharing their experiences.

National Childbirth Trust (NCT)
Alexandra House
Oldham Terrace
Acton
London W3 6NH
Tel: 0807 770 3236
NCT breastfeeding helpline:
0870 444 8708
www.nctpregnancyandbabycare.com
Provides support for pregnancy, birth
and early parenthood, and gives
information to enable parents to make
informed choices.

National Eczema Society
Hill House
Highgate Hill
London N19 5NA
Helpline: 0870 241 3604
www.eczema.org

NHS Direct
Tel: 0845 4647
www.nhsdirect.nhs.uk

NSPCC (National Society for the Prevention of Cruelty to Children)
42 Curtain Road
London EC2A 3NH
Free confidential helpline:
0808 800 5000
Tel: 0207 825 2500
www.nspcc.org.uk
UK's leading charity specializing in child
protection and the prevention of cruelty
to children.

Parentline Plus
Unit 520, Highgate Studios
53–57 Highgate Road
London
NW5 1TL
Helpline: 0808 800 2222
www.parentlineplus.org.uk
Offers support and information to
anyone parenting a child.

Royal Society for the Prevention of Accidents (RoSPA)
Edgbaston Park
353 Bristol Road
Edgbaston
Birmingham B5 7ST
Tel: 0121 248 2000
www.rospa.com
Offers general safety information,
advice and training.

St John Ambulance
27 St John's Lane
London EC1M 4BU
Tel: 08700 104 950
www.sja.org.uk
Provides first-aid training and services
in the UK.

TAMBA (Twins and Multiple Births Association)
2 The Willows
Gardner Road
Guildford GU1 4PG
Tel: 0870 770 3305
Helpline: 01732 868 000
www.tamba.org.uk
Encourages and offers support
to families and carers of twins,
triplets or more.

Vegan Society
Donald Watson House
7 Battle Road
St Leonards-on-Sea
East Sussex TN37 7AA
Tel: 01424 427 393
www.vegansociety.com

Vegetarian Society
Parkdale
Dunham Road
Altrincham
Cheshire WA14 4QG
Tel: 0161 925 2000
www.vegsoc.org

Index

Acknowledgments

Senior editors Julia North, Salima Hirani
Senior art editor Hannah Moore
Project editors Angela Baynham,
Anne Esden, Esther Ripley
Project art editors Claire Legemah,
Tracy Miles, Alison Tumer, Ann Burnham
Designer Iona Hoyle
DTP designer Julian Dams
Production controller Shwe Zin Win
Managing editor Liz Coghill
Managing art editors Emma Forge, Glenda Fisher
Photography art direction Sally Smallwood
Photography Ruth Jenkinson
Publishing manager Anna Davidson

Publishing director Corinne Roberts

Text by Eileen Hayes, Tracey Godridge, Katy Holland,
James Law and Joanna Moorhead.

Dorling Kindersley would like to thank Alyson Lacewing
for proofreading, Sue Bosanko for the index and Isabella
Jones for editorial assistance.

Picture credits
Dorling Kindersley would like to thank the following for
their kind permission to reproduce their photographs:
10 Mother & Baby Picture Library, Ian Hooton (tr);
12 Mother & Baby Picture Library, Ruth Jenkinson (tl);
13 Bubbles, Angela Hampton (br); 28 Mother & Baby
Picture Library, Ruth Jenkinson; 67 Mother & Baby
Picture Library, Eddie Lawrence (t); 69 Mother & Baby
Picture Library, Ian Hooton (t); 132 Science Photo
Library: Mark Clarke (bl).

All other images © Dorling Kindersley.
For further information see: www.dkimages.com